STEALING ELECTIONS, AMERICAN STYLE

STEALING ELECTIONS, AMERICAN STYLE

DAVID F. WALBERT

BLOOMSBURY ACADEMIC
NEW YORK • LONDON • OXFORD • NEW DELHI • SYDNEY

BLOOMSBURY ACADEMIC
Bloomsbury Publishing Inc, 1359 Broadway, New York, NY 10018, USA
Bloomsbury Publishing Plc, 50 Bedford Square, London, WC1B 3DP, UK
Bloomsbury Publishing Ireland, 29 Earlsfort Terrace, Dublin 2, D02 AY28, Ireland

BLOOMSBURY, BLOOMSBURY ACADEMIC and the Diana logo are trademarks of Bloomsbury Publishing Plc

First published in the United States of America 2026

Illustration: Nick Taylor

Library of Congress Cataloging-in-Publication Data

ISBN: HB: 979-8-216-39199-9
ePDF: 979-8-216-39200-2
eBook: 979-8-216-39201-9

Typeset by RefineCatch Limited, Bungay, Suffolk
Printed and bound in the United States of America

For product safety related questions contact productsafety@bloomsbury.com.
To find out more about our authors and books visit www.bloomsbury.com and sign up for our newsletters.

CONTENTS

ACKNOWLEDGMENTS AND DEDICATION

I am indebted to many people for the experiences that enabled me to write *Stealing Elections, American Style*. Among them are the hundreds of men and women I knew and represented, people like Curtis Thomas who had to quit school in the sixth grade to help his parents feed their family, and people like Herman Lodge who grew up when the Black schools in his county closed in the Fall to ensure that cheap labor would be available to pick cotton for white farmers. Herbert Phipps is an African American lawyer and judge who was born in "Bad Baker" County in South Georgia. Herb and I went to law school together and have been fast friends ever since. I learned a lot from Herb, some about racism in the South but more about what gives a person character and how to live your life in the face of adversity.

I was fortunate to count John Lewis as a friend and colleague. We often talked about his experiences in the Civil Rights Movement, the good and bad of American politics, and John once was a key witness for me in a voting case that ultimately went to the Supreme Court.

I also owe a debt of gratitude to those legislators, governors, members of Congress, and civil rights lawyers I worked with in the struggle to bring justice to the country's election laws. Progress was possible because of certain judges, the greatest of them being Earl Warren, Thurgood Marshall, and William Brennan on the Supreme Court, followed by Elbert Tuttle and John Minor Wisdom on the Fifth Circuit Court of Appeals. Chief Justice Warren was retired by the time I became a lawyer but his imprint on the nation was tremendous. I had the pleasure of arguing cases before the others.

I am grateful to Lilith Dorko, Bloomsbury's Senior Editor for U.S. Politics, Policy, and Security. Her encouragement and support since she first read the proposal for *Stealing Elections, American Style* made it easy to write the book. And I am grateful to my agent, Rita Rosenkranz, for introducing me to Lilith. My student research assistants, Sanya Kaushal and Zoya Bundukwala, were a pleasure to work with and one day will make their mark as inspired lawyers.

I could not have written this book had I not spent thousands of hours over forty years trying every imaginable kind of election case, from complicated constitutional cases that went to the Supreme Court to routine election contests. I taught constitutional law for a few years at Emory Law School when I was a young lawyer, but "doing the law" is where I learned how the Constitution works, or fails to work. Between the election cases and my "regular" litigation practice where I mostly earned my living, I worked long hours, and I am forever thankful to my wife Charlotte and our three sons, David, Chris, and Michael, for their loving understanding and support during all those years. I thank them too for the comments they made from time to time about this book and how to present its story. I am a lucky lawyer to have enjoyed the experiences I did while bringing some justice to the people I represented, but I am an even luckier father and husband.

PREFACE

If you thought this was a book of fiction—maybe a dramatic tale about conspirators stealing an election—you would be half right. *Stealing Elections, American Style* does indeed tell dramatic stories of people stealing elections, but there is not a word of fiction in it. And, as is often the case, truth is much stranger than fiction. The stories in these pages are more outlandish than anything a novelist would have the audacity to make up. They are gripping tales, but each one is also a dire warning.

Election fraud of every conceivable kind has occurred throughout the country's history. There's been ballot box stuffing, "losing" ballots, buying votes, erasing qualified voters from the rolls, the dead rising to vote, fake election returns, and on and on. If you include sheriffs, county commissioners, and all the local races, the number of elections stolen would be sobering. No one really knows what that number is, and this book doesn't try to answer that question.

What it does is tell the stories of some of the country's most important stolen elections, several of which changed the course of history. These stories of specific elections are woven together with chapters that explain the country's history of stealing elections with an endless litany of schemes and tricks. *Stealing Elections, American Style* brings that history up to date with recent presidential elections, voter suppression strategies, and an explanation of what is likely to happen under the Trump administration.

The notorious fraudulent presidential election of 1876 is the book's first chapter. Samuel J. Tilden beat Rutherford B. Hayes at the polls, but his victory was stolen by a fantastic web of partisan corruption. What began with one man's brazen act the night of the election mushroomed into a nationwide conspiracy. As Tilden later lamented, "The men who were elected by the people

President and Vice President of the United States were 'counted out,' and men who were not elected were 'counted in' and seated." The fraudulent vote count was so egregious the country nearly erupted in another civil war.

If you think the Supreme Court would step in to stop an election theft like that today, think again. The votes of Supreme Court justices were key to taking the presidency from Tilden—and their votes had nothing to do with the law and everything to do with their political party. One hundred fifty years later, little has changed. Partisan affiliation has been a near-perfect predictor of justices' votes in every case that involved a presidential candidate's claim to the office. Only two justices have ever voted contrary to their party affiliation—David Souter and John Paul Stevens, who dissented in *Bush v. Gore* in 2000.

Tilden anguished over what his election defeat meant for the future. With the country's ideal of honest elections and a peaceful transfer of power shattered, he predicted that corrupt elections for high office would be more likely. He was prescient, as later chapters show. Georgia's infamous Three Governor Controversy in 1947 saw Herman Talmadge's supporters shoot up the state capitol to slow ballot counting while others drove off in the middle of the night to "find" more votes—two months after the election. Other chapters take a close look at the 2000 and 2020 presidential elections and how the candidates, their campaigns, and their lawyers worked to steal those elections—successfully in the former instance and frighteningly close in the latter.

Outright fraud is only one way to steal an election, though. Vastly more elections are stolen before a single ballot is cast through rules that predetermine the outcome. *Stealing Elections, American Style* explains the many ways in which elections have been manipulated by gerrymandering, voter suppression, and election laws that stack the deck—methods that are more reliable than outright fraud. Rigging elections by manipulating the rules is the invisible but powerful machinery of election theft.

Throughout American history, those in power have used laws and voting procedures to shape the electorate to their advantage. Property ownership requirements once barred people from voting or holding office, and women were excluded from the ballot box for the first 150 years of the country's existence. Poll taxes, white-only primaries, bogus literacy tests given to Black voters, and other tricks kept African Americans out of politics for a century after the Civil War. When they were finally able to vote, their influence was blunted by other means.

Drawing districts to favor or exclude certain voters has been a part of American politics since Massachusetts Governor Elbridge Gerry's infamous "gerrymander" in 1812. In recent years, though, gerrymandering has become even more pernicious. Advances in data and mapping software have allowed political operatives to carve up districts so that elections are decided before the first vote is cast. The result is a political landscape where few districts are competitive, and elected officials choose their voters instead of voters choosing their representatives.

The gerrymander wars started by President Trump in 2025 have dragged partisan politics to a new low. But unless political gerrymandering is reigned in, redistricting after the 2030 census will be even worse. New methods of artificial intelligence that can exploit vast amounts of voter-specific data will enable mapmakers to draw districts with ever greater sophistication to lock in political control and lock opposition voters out of power.

I saw firsthand how election laws unfairly dictate winners when I tried my first voting case against Albany, Georgia, in 1975. Fresh out of law school and new to the state, it didn't take long to see that something was very wrong with Georgia's elections. African Americans were over a quarter of the state's population but accounted for fewer than 1 percent of the elected officials. The reason was obvious, and Albany epitomized the problem. Each of the city's seven commissioners was elected by all of the city's voters, allowing the white majority to elect white candidates to every position even though Black residents made up 35 percent of the population. It was the same story across the South. The remedy was simple—elect the commissioners by districts.

Given Albany's ironclad housing segregation, that would give African Americans a majority in at least two districts.

I won that case and, for the first time *ever*, Black commissioners were elected to the Albany City Commission. Over the next four decades, I litigated cases involving racial discrimination, political gerrymandering, malapportionment, what constitutes a racially fair district, the power of Congress to regulate voting, voter suppression, and election fraud. I testified before Congress on voting legislation and tried cases that went to the Supreme Court. Those are the experiences that inspired me to write this book, as I watched the country turning its back on voting rights and regressing to an old way of thinking—that *stealing elections is okay.*

I saw a lot of progress during the years I litigated cases, but progress was never a straight line. There were steps backward as well. One of the most disheartening was the Supreme Court's abandonment of the law to serve the justices' personal politics in the 2000 presidential election. Chapter 6—'The Bush–Gore Election: A Bloodless Coup'—tells what really happened in that election, from Florida's manipulation of the vote before the polls ever opened to the final decision of the Supreme Court on December 12, 2000.

The rights of voters have been more and more under assault for the last twenty years. Attacks come from the states, local governments, and most recently the federal government. To understand the present and see at least a little way into the future, one has to know history—what happened, why it happened, and what might have been done to make that history better. Two chapters explain the country's history of vote suppression. One of them addresses vote suppression during the first two centuries, and the other tells exactly what's going on today. Another chapter gives the history of drawing districts to control elections and again brings that history up to the present.

I believe the Supreme Court has played a much bigger role in our history of voting rights—mostly for the worse, unfortunately—than most people realize. I explain why that is true by looking at both old and recent cases where the court sent the country in the wrong direction, and a few under the leadership of Earl Warren where voting rights flourished for the benefit of the country and democratic ideals.

The battle over voting rights is never over. The tactics evolve, but one thing is constant: power. Whether through blatant fraud, judicial rulings, or quiet manipulation of election laws, those in control look for ways to stack the deck.

Stealing Elections, American Style is about the heart of the country's democracy—fair elections. Today's battles over election integrity, ballot access, and fair representation are the latest chapters in a long saga of people manipulating elections for political ends and others trying to stop them. The fight is different today, though, in one important respect. For the first time in the country's history, the federal government is a leader in the fight *against* voting rights and fair elections.

A recent case condemned the Trump administration's practice of punishing people for their views in violation of the First Amendment. The judge ended his order with these words:

> I fear President Trump believes the American people are so divided that today they will not stand up, fight for, and defend our most precious constitutional values so long as they are lulled into thinking their own personal interests are not affected.

The judge's comments apply equally to the current threats to our elections. Will we learn from our history and build a stronger democracy based on fair, honest elections—or will we repeat the mistakes of the past?

Which future we write is up to us.

1

Tilden–Hayes and the Stolen Presidency of 1876

The 1876 presidential election is shocking for its flagrant fraud. That shouldn't be surprising. The intense bitterness, resentment, and outright hatred that cleaved the country then makes today's schisms look mild.

It was only a decade since the Civil War left some 700,000 soldiers dead and wiped out an astounding 30 percent of the adult white male population in the South. Few on either side had survived the war without losing friends or family. The regional animosities that led to secession were anything but extinguished, and the indignation of defeat added to Southerners' historic resentment of Northern domination. Whether the country could choose a president peacefully and remain one country was a question with no certain answer. The previous four presidential elections—1860, 1864, 1868, and 1872—were not encouraging. The 1860 election of Lincoln triggered secession two weeks later. In each election from 1864 through 1872, Republican victories were achieved only by military occupation of Southern states and the disfranchisement of white Southerners who had supported the Confederacy.

With white disenfranchisement and the demographics of slavery, Black voters outnumbered white voters in parts of the South. Most African Americans voted for Republicans, of course, since the party of Lincoln was responsible for the end of slavery. They were joined by some white Southerners and by

Northern carpetbaggers who came south after the war, some well intended, others corrupt opportunists, and together elected Republican governments that held power thanks to occupying federal troops.

Those Reconstruction governments were anathema to many Southern whites, most of whom were Democrats who wanted to "Redeem" their world and recover the political power they once had. By the 1876 election, federal troops had been withdrawn from all but three Southern states—South Carolina, Louisiana, and Florida—and conservative Democrats had taken over the governments in the Redeemed states. For Democrats, the most important issue in the election was removing the stain of the last occupying troops. To Northern Republicans, keeping the national government out of the hands of the party that had split the Union was essential. Passion was fierce on both sides, so much so that many feared the election could trigger another civil war.

Ohio Governor Rutherford B. Hayes was the Republican candidate. He was temperate in his public remarks but knew that sectional passion and reminding Union veterans of their sacrifices—"waving the bloody shirt"—were the best way to get Republican votes, and he encouraged others to do exactly that when campaigning. Robert Ingersoll, a past Illinois Attorney General and eloquent speaker, was a master of the bloody shirt speech. He told his audiences why he opposed Democrats in spellbinding speeches that could last for two hours:

> Every State that seceded from the United States was a Democratic State. Every man that endeavored to tear the old flag from the heaven that it enriches was a Democrat. Every man that tried to destroy this nation was a Democrat . . .
>
> Every man that loved slavery better than liberty was a Democrat. The man that assassinated Abraham Lincoln was a Democrat. Every man that wanted the privilege of whipping another man to make him work for him for nothing and pay him with lashes on his naked back, was a Democrat.

> Every man that raised bloodhounds to pursue human beings was a Democrat. Every man that clutched from shrieking, shuddering, crouching mothers, babes from their breasts, and sold them into slavery, was a Democrat. . . . Every man that cursed Abraham Lincoln because he issued the Proclamation of Emancipation—the grandest paper since the Declaration of Independence—every one of them was a Democrat.[1]

Ingersoll's audiences both yelled for blood and wept. Democratic invective was equally fierce. The party platform demanded the end of the "rapacity of carpetbag tyrannies in the South."

Voters cared about two other big issues in 1876, and both hurt Hayes. The incumbent president, Republican Ulysses S. Grant, had just begun his second term when the Panic of 1873 exploded and caused widespread bankruptcies, bank failures, and unemployment. Largely as a result of the Panic, Republicans lost ninety-two congressional seats in the 1874 election, turning a big Republican majority into a dominant Democratic majority of 182 seats to 103. The Panic still gripped the country in 1876.

The Grant administration was also rocked by scandal and corruption, and Hayes' campaign was dragged down by the stench of Republican corruption even though he was not implicated personally. Moreover, the Democratic candidate, New York Governor Samuel J. Tilden, had an auspicious record of anti-corruption reform. When he was chairman of the New York State Democratic Party, Tilden went after the spectacularly corrupt Boss Tweed who had stolen billions of dollars, in today's money, from New York City taxpayers.

Most people thought Tilden would win on November 7, and what was expected played out on election night. The returns showed that Tilden won the popular vote by over 250,000, a healthy 3 percent advantage. Tilden was also garnering a majority of the electoral votes, carrying several Northern states that had been uncertain. The Redeemed Southern states were expected to go for Tilden, and they all did. Only in the three Southern states that still had

Reconstruction governments were the results close, but on election night Tilden was reported to have won those as well.

Even without any of those three states, Tilden had 184 electoral votes, just one short of a majority, and the state Republican Party chairmen had conceded the election in both Louisiana and Florida. Zachariah Chandler, the national Republican Chairman, closed the New York campaign headquarters when he realized Hayes had lost. Both candidates went to bed with the same understanding. The next morning, newspaper headlines based on the returns from election night announced Tilden's victory.

Unbeknownst to the candidates and newspapers, however, one man didn't accept the results. Daniel E. Sickles was the perfect man to try the impossible, stealing the presidential election. He was a rogue with a long history of outlandish, dishonest behavior. As a New York state senator, he was censured for bringing a prostitute onto the floor of the legislature. He was later elected to Congress but soon became embroiled in an even more notorious scandal. When Sickles learned that his wife was having an affair with the Attorney General of the District of Columbia—Philip Key II, son of Francis Scott Key—he confronted the unarmed Key in Lafayette Square and declared, "You must die." Sickles pulled his pistol and fired, knocking Key down. As Key begged for his life, Sickles fired twice more, killing him. Though the shooting was plainly premeditated, Sickles was acquitted. Then, in the Civil War, Sickles' service as a brigadier general was tarnished when he twisted events to make himself out a hero.

As the 1876 election approached, Sickles hoped Hayes would win partly because of his disdain for Tilden's tepid support for the Union during the war, and partly because he was short of funds and hoped to receive an appointment from a Hayes administration. Late on election night, Sickles went by Republican National Committee headquarters and found the place deserted except for a clerk who told Sickles that everyone had left when they realized Tilden had won. The Republican Chairman was upstairs in his hotel room with a bottle of liquor to console himself. Sickles looked over the election returns and saw that

Tilden was reported to have won the three unredeemed Southern states by relatively small margins. But Sickles knew that loyal Republicans controlled the election boards in those states and they would do almost anything to keep their states in Republican hands.

In a brazen act that only someone like Sickles would even have thought of, he drafted telegrams to the Republican governors of the three states and directed them not to acknowledge Tilden's victory. He told each of them that all Hayes needed to win the presidency was to carry their state. In fact, Hayes could win only if he took the nineteen electoral votes of all three states, but that was trivial sleight of hand compared to Sickles' big objective—getting the election returns reversed. The exact words of the telegrams were: "With your state sure for Hayes, he is elected. Hold your state."[2] At Sickles instructions, the clerk sent the telegrams out under the name of the Republican National Chairman, and a fuse was lit that would burn down the façade of democracy and nearly burn down the country again.

Sickles' bold ploy caught fire immediately. South Carolina Governor Daniel Chamberlain telegraphed a response at 3 a.m. confirming he was on board: "All right. South Carolina is for Hayes." Republicans in Louisiana also took Sickles' cue and claimed Hayes had won there even though the vote totals said the opposite by a wide margin. The Associated Press soon reported both sides were claiming victory in Florida.

Editors at the *New York Times*, a staunch Republican paper, met on the morning of November 8 to decide how to portray Hayes' loss. One of those editors, John C. Reid, detested Democrats and couldn't abide a Tilden presidency. He had been a prisoner at Andersonville where 13,000 Union soldiers died in atrocious conditions. Reid badgered the other editors until they agreed to report the election as "in doubt" rather than a Tilden win. The *Times* story immediately gained a life of its own.

Many prominent Republicans who believed Tilden had won nevertheless announced a Hayes victory, a false claim that reverberated across the nation in the headlines of partisan newspapers. Hayes himself continued to believe that Tilden had won. Encouraged to claim victory regardless, he declined. Similarly, Tilden was asked to denounce Republican fraud and hint that force would be used if necessary to keep his victory, but he kept his comments mild. Millions on both sides believed their candidate had won, and threats of civil war resonated throughout the country. Talk that Democrats were arming for a march on Washington to ensure Tilden became president were serious enough that President Grant ordered additional soldiers to guard the federal arsenal.

Both campaigns sent teams to Tallahassee, New Orleans, and Columbia for the expected donnybrook over the states' electoral votes. Throngs of reporters swamped all three capitals, and their daily stories kept the country boiling. No one believed election laws alone would carry the day with the state canvassing boards that were responsible for declaring the results. Politics would be at least as important. Promises of favor to board members and outright bribery were widely feared, too. The facts may have favored Tilden, but state politics very much favored Hayes, just as Sickles expected. Bribery could work in favor of either side. William E. Chandler, a longtime leader of the Republican Party and a railroad lobbyist, brought $10,000 in cash when he went to New Orleans.

The state boards had four weeks before the Electoral College would meet on December 6, and the evidence of election fraud that poured out over those four weeks was astounding. As soon as the polls closed, votes started shifting from Tilden to Hayes.

The South Carolina Canvassing Board was the first of the three boards to convene, and it promptly degenerated into anarchy driven by state politics. Wade Hampton, the Democratic nominee for governor, opposed Chamberlin who was running for re-election. Chamberlin, a carpetbagger from Massachusetts, was reviled by Democrats but had also lost favor with many people, Black and white, who had voted Republican before. Hampton aggressively campaigned for Black support, endorsed equal voting rights for African Americans, and condemned election violence of any sort, all of which led to significant Democratic support among Black voters.

In spite of the protestations of people like Hampton, vote fraud in South Carolina occurred on an epic scale and in every way imaginable—individuals casting multiple ballots; polls blocked; mismarked ballots tricking voters; vote buying; and intimidation of voters and poll officials. Both parties cheated, the Democrats especially so in the state's western counties. Of the three states, South Carolina saw the most pre-election violence—Democrats against Republicans and Republicans against Democrats (Black Republicans were angry at African Americans who supported Democrats)—though white Democrats surely were the greater offenders. Notwithstanding the racism and violence of the time, Black voters in South Carolina still outnumbered white voters in 1876.

The South Carolina Canvassing Board had five members, all Republicans. The county returns the board received showed Hampton ahead for governor by over a thousand votes and Hayes ahead by several hundred. The returns also showed that the legislature, which was majority Republican, had flipped to a Democratic majority. That was important not just for legislative control, but because the legislature determined which gubernatorial candidate, Hampton or Chamberlain, won in case of a dispute. That put the Republican canvassing board in a quandary. Throwing out some of the returns to maintain a Republican majority in the legislature would open the door to Democrats challenging counties that had given Hayes fraudulent votes.

Democrats immediately sued the board in the South Carolina Supreme Court, which ordered it to tally the reported returns exactly as reported by the counties. Undaunted, the board ignored the Supreme Court and went ahead and threw out enough precincts to let Republicans hold their majority in the legislature. At the same time the board refused to hear similar fraud allegations by Democrats that would have given the state to Tilden. The board members were promptly arrested and jailed for violating the court's order. With the canvassing board in jail, the elections went from weird to completely whacky. A federal judge interceded and ruled that the board had acted legally, freeing the jailed board members. That judge's ruling was lawless, but the law had already fallen far behind politics. The judge was a Republican appointee.

The state government tied itself in knots. Both Hampton and Chamberlain claimed to be the true governor, and two separate groups claimed to be the duly elected legislature. The two-governor controversy created a huge problem for the presidential election. Who had authority to name South Carolina's delegates to the Electoral College? The U.S. Constitution does not specify any procedure for choosing electors; it assigns that responsibility to the states to decide on their own.

Naturally, Chamberlain claimed authority as the last person to hold the office of governor, and he issued certificates to seven Republican electors. A contrary certificate in favor of Tilden was submitted by the Democratic legislature. If the Tilden certificate was honored, he would be president.

In Florida, pre-election misconduct was "typical" of the era—there was lots of money to buy votes, and some employers controlled how their workers voted. The Florida Central Railroad gave its employees numbered ballots marked for the Democratic candidates with the understanding that each person's numbered slip better show up in the ballot box. That could be done in 1876 because voting by secret ballot was still years in the future. The Republican-controlled Jacksonville, Pensacola & Mobile Railroad fired employees who attended Democratic events, and the Florida Superintendent of Public Education, a Republican, urged Black voters to vote "early and often," an admonishment that elicits a laugh today but was dead serious in 1876.

The Florida Canvassing Board had three members, Secretary of State Samuel McLin, Comptroller Clayton Cowgill, and Attorney General William Cocke. McLin and Cowgill were loyal Republicans. Cocke was an independent-minded Democrat who had broken ranks to support Grant in the 1872 election. Like South Carolina, Florida's presidential politics and the vote count were complicated by the governor's race where Democrat George Drew ran against the Republican incumbent, Marcellus Stearns.

When the Canvassing Board opened the returns from the county boards, heavily Democratic Baker County was reported for Hayes, a surprise to almost everyone. In fact, Baker County's voters had cast their ballots for Tilden, but Governor Stearns had replaced all the men on the county's election board three days after the election. The new county board members, all Republican officeholders, had held back the votes from two Baker County precincts that were strong for Tilden and Drew. When that came to light, even the Republicans on the Florida Canvassing Board agreed the fraud had to be corrected, and that correction gave Tilden a ninety-four-vote victory statewide.

The reported vote, of course, was not the end of the game in Florida any more than it was in South Carolina. The Republican majority on the Canvassing Board, over Cocke's objection, threw out 2,000 votes from Democratic precincts, just enough to give Stearns a majority in the governor's race and flip the presidential results, putting Hayes back ahead of Tilden. On December 6, Stearns signed a certificate to the Electoral College naming four Hayes electors. Cocke, as both Attorney General and a member of the Florida Canvassing Board, signed a separate certificate with four Tilden electors. There was plenty of evidence that the Florida board's vote was for sale, but no direct evidence ever surfaced that a bribe was actually paid.

Democrats challenged the board's decision, but Republicans weren't worried because two of the three justices on the Florida Supreme Court were Republicans who they counted on. They were astounded when the decision turned out to be a rare exception—a ruling based on the law rather than the justices' political party. All three justices agreed that the board could determine what votes had actually been cast, as it did in Baker County, but it had no authority to adjudicate whether votes were legal. That was a judicial function that only a court could perform.[3] Applying that rule to the presidential race, Tilden should receive Florida's electoral votes, but no one knew if the court's ruling would be followed in Washington. The court's decision came on December 22, two weeks after the Electoral College met, but two months before electoral certificates were to be opened in Congress.

As crooked as the elections were in South Carolina and Florida, they were pristine compared to Louisiana. The presidential election was complicated again by a gubernatorial election. Francis Nicholls, the Democratic nominee, was a well-liked native of Louisiana. He had been so badly wounded in the Civil War that he drew sympathy from Republicans as well as Democrats, Blacks as well as whites. Nicholls lost an arm at Shenandoah Valley, his left foot was shot off at Chancellorsville, and he lost an eye while commanding a group of invalid soldiers. Like Wade Hampton, Nicholls reached out to Black voters.

The Republican candidate was Stephen Packard, a thirty-seven-year-old native of Maine who first set foot in Louisiana as a captain in the Union Army and had made plenty of enemies in his own party. He had been nominated at a deeply fractured convention that collapsed into screaming, fist fights, and drawn pistols. Some Republican newspapers praised Packard, but the Democratic papers were ruthless. The *New Orleans Democrat* denounced him as "adding the prejudices of birth and sectional hate to the venom of party greed and personal ambition."[4]

Much of the ire directed at Packard came from his being U.S. Marshal, which gave him influence over the New Orleans Custom House that controlled tremendous wealth and had been a source of corruption throughout Reconstruction. Packard was widely accused of helping President Grant's brother skim vast sums from the Custom House, costing the state tax revenue that was supposed to go to public schools.

Democratic leaders were sensitive to voting intimidation since they didn't want to give the Louisiana Returning Board any excuse for throwing out votes like they had done before to give Republican candidates a win. That did not mean there was no election violence in Louisiana, but it was much less than in earlier years, and what happened was often disputed. In one notorious incident, a Black man named Henry Pinkston was murdered in his home, and Pinkston's widow claimed that thirty or forty white men shot him while accusing him of being a Republican. The day after the murder, however, she said that a group of Black men had killed him, and neighbors reported that she herself had murdered several people and had threatened to kill her husband many times.

Election skullduggery occurred on both sides, but Republican control of both the federal and state governments gave them opportunities to steal the election at every point. The parish election clerks acted like Republican campaign operatives. Democratic requests for just one clerk in each office were rejected. The Republican Party went so far as to send a letter to each election supervisor telling them exactly how many Republican votes they needed to produce and reminding them that their post-election rewards would depend on "doing [their] full duty."[5]

The "Southern Sewing Machine" swindle was an especially brazen scam. Republicans arranged to have fake flyers delivered by the post office to 29,000 registered Democrats in New Orleans right before the election. The federal post office was controlled by Republicans, of course, and Republican mail carriers were told to return every flier where the addressee wasn't found at home. Arrest warrants were then issued against thousands of people for false voter registration based on the retuned fliers, and 8,000 legitimate Democratic voters were removed from the registration list with no time to be reinstated before the election—an enormous fraud in an election with only 160,000 votes cast statewide.[6]

Even with Republican cheating, Democrats thought they would win, and they seemed to be right on election night. Tilden was ahead by nearly 8,000 votes and Nicholls by a bit more, huge leads that should hold even in Louisiana. Still, there was the Louisiana Returning Board which consisted of four Republicans with dubious reputations. The board's chair, Madison Wells, had stitched together a uniquely opportunistic political career, changing sides whenever it was to his advantage. He fought on both sides in the Civil War, was elected lieutenant governor as a Republican, then governor as a Democrat. He switched parties again in 1872 to support President Grant's re-election bid and was appointed to the returning board the next year. Board member Thomas Anderson was blunt about the board's intentions. He told a friend, "They may beat us voting, but we have the best of them in the count."[7]

Whether the board members were bribed remains unknown to history, but there was plenty of proof that they were available for the right price. Wells told one Democrat that $200,000 to both himself and Anderson plus some lesser sums to the board's two Black members would do the job. Wells later admitted the conversation; he just denied that he initiated the offer. Wells also sent a friend, Maddox, to Washington to arrange a bribe. Maddox quoted a price of $1 million when he got to D.C. but got no takers. Wells' denial of that initiative fell apart when a letter came to light that Wells had given to Maddox to deliver to Republican Senator J. R. West during Maddox's Washington trip. The letter reeked of bribery. Wells told West that "millions have been sent here" to be used for Tilden, and it would be impossible for Wells to blunt those millions without "some countermove." He closed with a thinly failed threat: "See our friends and act promptly or results will be disastrous. A hint to the wise."[8]

Bribed or not, the board was a partisan farce. It met in secret when it wanted to conceal its worst and ignored repeated requests to allow Democratic representation on the board. It wouldn't even allow a Democratic clerk to observe the tallying of parish returns, which was all done in secret. In a flagrant conflict of interest, the board's lawyer, who attended its secret meetings, was also counsel to the Republican Party.

By throwing out heavily Democratic precincts, the board eliminated 13,211 Tilden votes while costing Hayes only 2,412 votes. A Tilden majority of nearly 8,000 became a Hayes majority of 3,437.[9] Using that contrived vote count, Republican Governor William Kellog certified Louisiana's eight electors for Hayes. Refusing to succumb to the fraud, John McEnery—the Democratic candidate for governor in the previous election—certified a list of eight

Democratic electors. McEnery claimed he was the rightful current governor because the returning board had stolen his election too.

Beyond the three Southern states, what had been a minor distraction in Oregon suddenly became critical. Oregon was carried by Hayes, but one of his electors, John Watts, was a federal officer which disqualified him from being an elector. In place of Watts, Oregon's Governor La Fayette Grover, a Democrat, certified as the third elector the candidate who received the next highest number of votes, E. A. Cronin, who was a Tilden supporter. That terrified Republicans, since Tilden would be president if Hayes lost a *single one* of Oregon's electoral votes even if Hayes took all the disputed Southern votes. Desperate, Watts resigned his federal post, and the other Republican electors "appointed" Watts to replace himself. They then submitted electoral certificates that had been signed earlier by Oregon's secretary of state before Watts' disqualification was known.

Oregon created a big problem for Republicans. To win all three of Oregon's votes, Congress would have to go behind Governor Grover's certification of the state's electors, but winning the electoral votes of the three Southern states required the opposite—the certificates from the sitting governors needed to be treated as conclusive. If Republicans could challenge the certificate from Oregon's governor as illegal, Democrats should likewise be allowed to challenge the Southern states' certificates as fraudulent.

Democrats seethed as they watched what was happening. The dishonesty of the Louisiana Board was so obvious and extreme that it risked war. Indiana Democrats telegraphed their Louisiana counterparts that a half million men were ready to fight. Calls to arms were heard across the country, sounding frighteningly like what had preceded secession a decade earlier.

Tilden finally denounced the unfolding fraud. "Our presidential election has been subverted by a false count of the votes cast by the presidential electors, founded on . . . pretended votes known at the time to be fraudulent or forged." With tempers at risk of boiling over, the House and Senate sent delegations to investigate. No doubt, many congressmen hoped to assuage the rising tide of anger, but bolstering their parties' claim to the presidency was a bigger spur to action.

Claiming "states' rights," the Louisiana Returning Board refused to be investigated by Congress. The congressional committees had to work with copies of whatever they could get. In a harbinger of what was to come, the congressional reports did nothing to subdue the controversy—they had the opposite effect. The report from the Democratic House of Representatives condemned the Louisiana Returning Board for having "entered upon the canvass . . . with a prearranged purpose to . . . fraudulently declare the result in favor of Hayes and Wheeler. [The Board] did not hesitate to commit any act of official perfidy necessary to the end to be attained."[10] Conversely, the minority House report by the Republican members praised the board and endorsed the Hayes electors. Similar reports were issued by the Senate committee, only reversed to reflect that the Senate was majority Republican. The reports hardened voters' views, both sides now having more to support their stand.

The Constitution wasn't clear as to exactly what should happen next. The Twelfth Amendment said that "The President of the Senate shall, in the presence of the Senate and House of Representatives, open all the certificates and the votes shall then be counted." Historically, once the certificates were opened, all the members of Congress, together, determined the electoral vote count. Because Republicans were a majority in the Senate but a minority in Congress overall, they were afraid to follow the historic procedure. Instead, they concocted an "interpretation" of the Twelfth Amendment that would give the President of the Senate—Republican Thomas Ferry of Michigan—the authority to not just open the certificates, but also to *count* the votes and *determine* which were the "right" ones when they were disputed.

Responding to that game, Democrats said the president should be chosen by the House alone if not by the entire Congress. Their position was more credible than the Republicans' tortured argument, since the Twelfth Amendment did empower the House alone to choose the president when no candidate won a majority of the electoral votes. If a single Hayes vote was excluded because of its irregularity (which Republicans had done to Southern electoral votes in two previous elections), the election would go to the House since no candidate had a majority of the electoral votes. Tilden would prevail there.

While the election fight played out in public, another drama was playing out in private. Monied interests had great influence in Congress, of course, and in 1876 there was no more fearsome political power than that wielded by the country's big railroads. Bribes in cash and company stock were commonplace, and congressmen's votes were often dictated by their railroad patrons. The Texas & Pacific Railroad was one of the most powerful, and it wanted legislation and subsidies to complete a Southern line to the Pacific. Thomas Scott was president of the Texas & Pacific and a man of notorious power over Congress. The Texas & Pacific was opposed by the Central Pacific Railroad, which wanted a Northern route from the Pacific to the east. Scott's opposite number at the Central Pacific was Collis Huntington, a California railroad baron whose political power was on a par with Scott's.

These two titans had been deadlocked with neither able to ram their plan through Congress over the other's opposition. But Scott saw the election crisis as an opportunity to get what he wanted by packaging together a solution to both problems, the presidency and his rail connection to the Pacific. State legislatures and newspapers in the South had endorsed the Texas & Pacific line because it favored Southern economic interests, and Scott had diligently curried Southern support. What became known as the Scott Plan would give the South the Southern line to the Pacific *plus* the removal of federal troops *and* other political rewards if Hayes became president. To make it work, Scott would have to induce enough Southern Democrats to relinquish a Tilden presidency.[11]

That seemed possible. The most strident cries demanding a Tilden presidency came from Northern Democrats. Even in Louisiana where federal troops were all that kept Packard's carpetbagger government afloat, there was relative peace. Two governors and two separate legislatures claimed authority—just as in South Carolina—but as bizarre as that was, Louisianans had lived through the same schizophrenic government after the last election. It was nothing to die over, especially when the nation's political tide was turning against Reconstruction, and Redemption seemed to be coming no matter who was president.

Scott thought he had the power to get his plan passed over Huntington's opposition, but he was wrong. When he realized that fact, he met with Huntington in late December and the two moguls struck a deal. They would use their collective influence over Congress to get most of what *both* railroads wanted. Scott would get the subsidies he wanted for the Texas & Pacific; Huntington would get federal subsidies, too, and also the right to build the western end of the rail line in California to join the Southern Pacific. That line had to be open to all carriers, though; it couldn't be monopolized. The political crisis would be resolved as Scott originally planned—Hayes would be president.

Hayes was not a supporter of any compromise at first, but then he learned that some Republican senators wouldn't support the ploy of Ferry counting the electoral votes by himself. Some also doubted that Hayes was entitled to the votes of Florida and Louisiana. Even President Grant expressed doubts about the Republican claim to Louisiana. Suddenly, the compromise looked very good to Hayes.

At the same time, the public mood had gone from ugly to explosive. By early January, there were calls to use whatever force was necessary to ensure a Tilden presidency. Secret organizations of Democrats preparing for war sprouted up in Northern and Western states. A large Democratic rally in Columbus, Ohio, resolved to take up arms if Ferry tried to count the electoral votes alone. The Democratic governor of Indiana put the state militia on a war footing. Republican Pennsylvania made counter preparations for war. Henry Watterson, a congressman and the editor of the *Louisville Courier-Journal*, was the loudest

Southern voice supporting what sounded like insurrection when he called for "at least ten thousand armed Kentuckians" to go to Washington on February 14 when electoral votes would be opened. In a speech on January 8, the Democrats' Jackson Day, Watterson called for 100,000 men to march on Washington to secure Tilden's election. Even the Sergeant-at-Arms of the House of Representatives proposed deputizing 100,000 men to ensure Tilden became president.

In the hope of defusing the public's anger, Congress created a bipartisan Electoral Commission on January 29 to determine the winner of the election. The authorizing legislation directed the Commission to use the "same powers, if any, now possessed by Congress" for determining a candidate's electoral votes. In effect, Congress told the Commission, "Do what Congress would do," which was not very encouraging given Congress' inability to move beyond purely partisan interests. The Commission couldn't make a binding allocation of electoral votes, but it was expected that Congress would ratify the Commission's decision.

The Commission had fifteen members. The Senate appointed three Republican and two Democratic senators, and the House appointed three of its Democratic members and two Republican members. The remaining five members were Supreme Court justices, two Republicans and two Democrats, and those four were to pick a fifth Supreme Court justice. It was assumed the fifth would be David Davis, the court's most independent member.

Democrats agreed to the Commission in large part because they didn't see another path that didn't lead to war. Republicans controlled the Senate, the presidency, and the army, where ultimate power resided. Southerners needed no reminder of that. Even if Democrats were able to get the question decided by the House and name Tilden president, that could lead to a war they would surely lose. Moreover, Democrats thought they had a strong case for the Commission, and Tilden only needed a single one of the twenty disputed electoral votes to win.

Democratic optimism about the Electoral Commission was suddenly shaken when the Illinois legislature elected Davis as a U.S. senator, preventing him from serving as the potential fifth justice on the Commission. The four justices already on the Commission then selected Republican Joseph Bradley (there were no other Democrats on the court) to fill the fifteenth seat on the Commission. Some Democrats despaired; others thought Bradley might have an independent streak, since he had recently voted to eviscerate Republicans' civil rights legislation. In any event they would find out very soon since the Commission had to act quickly with the date for the next president to take office fast approaching.

On February 7, the Commission met to announce its decision on Florida's electoral votes. If it simply followed the Florida Supreme Court ruling that the Florida Returning Board could not go past the face of the returns, Tilden would win. But when Bradley read his opinion, Democrats were apoplectic. All four of Florida's disputed electoral votes were awarded to Hayes as the Commission split on purely partisan lines—the eight Republicans voted for Hayes, the seven Democrats for Tilden. Any hope that the Commission's decisions would follow the law and the evidence was gone. Every other vote split the same way—eight Republicans to seven Democrats—and Hayes was awarded every contested electoral vote.

Allegations of corruption by the commissioners jumped off the front pages of the country's newspapers. Bradley had long been dogged by corruption allegations because of a tortured ruling in a railroad case that made Tom Scott yet another fortune. Bradley himself had become wealthy as a railroad lawyer before he was a judge and was accused of being Scott's puppet on the Commission. The public criticism of Bradley was so intense that he was forced to write a public denial about his conduct on the Commission, but conspicuously missing from his letter was any explanation of his relationship with Scott. Though it wasn't made public at the time, Tilden was told he could have the vote of one of the three Republican justices on the Commission for a price, and the offer insinuated that Bradley was the one.

Reports of Democratic governors preparing for war sprang up again after the Commission's rulings, and people who had thought the country was on a path to a peaceful resolution were despondent over the likelihood of violence. A bullet was fired into Hayes' house, and in New Orleans a Democrat from Pennsylvania shot and wounded Governor Packard. A Democratic newspaperman who wrote that Hayes might be shot as he walked to the Capitol to be inaugurated was indicted for sedition. President Grant ordered an ostentatious review of troops to remind people that violence would be met by the army.

When the Commission's Florida ruling was presented to Congress on February 10, frustrated Democrats threatened to prevent Congress from completing the electoral vote count in order to prevent Hayes becoming president. They hoped to force a new election. The House voted on a strict party line to recess until 12th, stopping any further counting of electoral votes. With the end of the 44th Session of Congress just three weeks away, the threat of repeated recesses to prevent a Hayes victory became very real. What days earlier had been a successful compromise that would save the nation from splintering was itself at risk of splintering. What was most troubling about the recess vote was that it had the support of Southern Democrats who were key to the compromise and delivering the presidency to Hayes.

The next weeks were among the most chaotic ever in Congress. Tempers flared and lobbyists packed the House floor. More recess motions were made and fought over, but they were defeated when most Southern Democrats rejoined Republicans to move forward. Still, many feared the compromise might fall apart, and Southern congressmen exacted more commitments to secure their support. President Grant acknowledged that Nicholls was the rightful governor of Louisiana, not Packard, a concession that would have been inconceivable weeks earlier. Hayes agreed to include Southerners in his cabinet and guaranteed that the South would be fairly treated in appropriations for internal improvements, which had not been the case before.

Even with the latest agreements, a peaceful resolution remained precarious, and the risk of falling into the abyss continued to hang over Congress. Just how precarious was dramatically shown when a minor editorial in an Ohio newspaper on February 22, just a week before the presidential clock ran out, threatened to explode the compromise. The editorial was a scathing criticism of Louisiana Democrats, very similar to hundreds of other articles and editorials that had appeared in Republican newspapers over the past year. But the editor of this paper was a close friend of Hayes, and people were ready to believe the editorial reflected Hayes' view of the South. In fact, the editor himself was not even aware the editorial was being published, much less did it reflect Hayes' views towards the South.

Regardless, the editorial gave an opening to those Democrats who hoped to squash any deal that would make Hayes president. Southerners who had been ready to vote for Hayes worried that they might be walking into a trap. Maybe, they wondered, Hayes would just be a Reconstruction president. Hayes' true colors were far from that, but their fears were compounded by the cries of their constituents. A motion for a recess to the next day carried, *and* it was supported by every one of the thirty Southern Democrats who had joined Republicans in opposing the last recess motion.

National chaos was only a few days away unless all the forces that had fashioned and nursed the compromise, the economic ones and the political ones, could convince the conflicted congressmen to hold the line. Help came on March 1 when Congressman William Levy of Louisiana rose to speak in the midst of the bedlam. He gave a ringing endorsement of what the South would see in a Hayes administration and asked all who wanted to "protect Louisiana and South Carolina" to join him in voting against the recess so the electoral count could be finished. Levy's dramatic speech undermined the recess strategy since he represented one of the two states that Northern Democrats were supposedly trying to help. After Levy sat down, another motion to recess failed, and the electoral vote count slogged on until the next morning. At 4 a.m. on

March 2, Hayes was finally declared the next president by a majority of one electoral vote.

In a fitting coda to the 1876 election, Hayes traveled from Ohio to Washington for his inauguration in a luxurious private railroad car. It was owned by the Pennsylvania Railroad and provided by Tom Scott.

In what was now only a symbolic act, Southern and Northern Democrats joined together to pass a resolution on March 3, one day before the 44th Congress ended, declaring that Tilden had won the election. They acted out of a mix of feelings—an honest belief that Tilden had won, disgust with the Election Commission, and concern for how their votes for Hayes looked to their constituents.

Tilden seldom made public comments about the election, but when he did, he minced no words: "Everybody knows that, after the recent election, the men who were elected President and Vice President of the United States were counted out, and men who were not elected were 'counted in' and seated." Tilden never showed any personal bitterness but spoke of the "four and a quarter million voters who were defrauded of the fruits of their elective franchise." He warned future generations what the stolen election of 1876 would mean for them:

> If the men in possession of the government can, in one instance, maintain themselves in power against an adverse decision at the elections, such an example will be imitated. Temptation always exists. Devices to give the color of law, and false pretenses on which to found fraudulent decisions, will not be wanting. The wrong will grow into a practice if once condoned.[12]

Tilden's words echo loudly a century and a half later.

2

When Georgia had Three Governors

The South has had far more than its share of outrageous political figures. Flamboyant populists ran by preying on those who felt left behind and blaming elites for their plight. The demagogues' fictional promises of something better went unfilled, but their song still resonated with voters who bristled with resentment. Most Southern demagogues traded on white fears of African Americans and assorted others—immigrants, Catholics, and communists have been popular targets.

Demagoguery and stealing elections went hand in hand since nothing was considered out of bounds to seize power. U.S. Senator "Pitchfork" Ben Tillman of South Carolina proudly admitted on the Senate floor that whites stuffed ballot boxes to keep Black voters from winning elections.[1] Mississippi Governor, and later Senator, Theodore Bilbo, "called on every red-blooded white man to use any means to keep the niggers away from the polls" when he ran for re-election in 1946.[2] Louisiana's Huey Long, who also served as governor and senator, was an equally flamboyant populist but didn't feed off the fires of racism. Long believed in actually helping poor people, not just bedazzling them to get their votes. "My program is for the poor man—regardless of color—to have enough to eat, to have decent clothes to wear, and a roof over his head." But Long was a relentless abuser of political office, and that ultimately led to his end. He was assassinated when he gerrymandered the assassin's father-in-law out of his elected office as punishment for some act of political disloyalty.

Georgia's unquestioned nominee for the rogue's gallery of Southern demagogues is Eugene Talmadge, aptly nicknamed the "Wild Man from Sugar Creek." He graduated from the University of Georgia with a law degree but moved to a farm his wife inherited in rural Telfair County. Talmadge didn't like grueling farm work and had little success as a lawyer in the county seat of McRae, population 1,200, but he was intoxicated with politics and ran for the state senate in 1922. He got a harsh lesson in dirty politics when the opposition accused Talmadge of buggering his mule.[3] Apparently mule-buggery was not a disqualification for political office in rural Georgia since Talmadge won the most votes in his three-county district. But he lost the election because he carried only one of the three counties and the winner was determined by the number of counties carried, not the number of votes won.

One would have had to have been clairvoyant to have predicted Talmadge's political future, but in retrospect, it's clear how all the pieces led to one of the most extraordinary election thefts in American history. Talmadge's last election had some of everything bad in it. The election was scarred by violence, racism, flagrant voter suppression, false claims of vote fraud (while real fraud was denied), ballot box stuffing, and a mob that overran the state capitol to stop the vote counting. When the votes were finally counted, three people claimed the right to be Georgia's governor in a tense, armed standoff between the National Guard and the State Guard, each loyal to a different man. None of it could have happened but for the kind of politician Talmadge was—a demagogue of the worst sort.

Talmadge's first statewide race was in 1926 for the Democratic nomination for agriculture commissioner. Winning the nomination was the same thing as winning the office outright, since there were so few Republicans in Georgia at the time that none ran for statewide office. Georgia also had a unique "county-unit" system for statewide primary elections that heavily favored rural voters. The primary winner was not the candidate who won the popular vote, but the winner of the most "county unit votes." Two unit votes were allocated to each of Georgia's 159 counties, no matter how few people lived there, and up to four additional unit votes, but no more, were allocated to the most populous counties. Under the county-unit system, each rural voter had vastly more clout than a city voter, so that winning their votes was more important than winning votes in Atlanta or other urban counties.

Statewide campaigning in Georgia in 1926 was largely person-to-person, meeting with the newspaperman in each town, stopping by the courthouse, and going to the general store to introduce yourself. "Mass communication" was speaking from the back of a buckboard wagon to as many people as could be gathered up, and Talmadge excelled in that theater. His target were poor farmers, though "poor" was redundant. All Georgia farmers were poor.

Talmadge raced around the state, speaking everywhere he could. He was a master of manipulating the emotions of a crowd and talked to the farmers in the kind of language that convinced them he would "take care of us." They became avid devotees who believed anything he said. The real showmen of that era were the itinerant tent preachers who took their revivals from town to town, and Talmadge was as much preacher and entertainer as politician. He wasn't religious, but he flowered his speeches with biblical aphorisms. The real Christian believers in his audience were convinced they were listening to a man of God. When the 1926 election was over, a new Georgia political power had been born. Talmadge handily beat the incumbent commissioner who most people had thought was sure to win re-election.

Talmadge ran the Agriculture Department impulsively and demanded absolute loyalty from his aids. He was also quick to ignore the law when it got in his way, but the farmers—his "wool hat boys," as poor dirt farmers were known—loved him. He was re-elected in 1928 and 1930, the last time with 72 percent of the popular vote and 98 percent of the county unit votes. Still,

Talmadge had more than a few enemies. Department funds were loosely accounted for, there were boondoggle trips to "study agriculture," his friends and family were notorious for having state cars for their personal use, and state funds had a habit of being deposited in banks owned by Talmadge's friends.

Then came the "great hog controversy." Knowing the governor would disapprove a request for funds if he asked, Talmadge ordered the State Bureau of Markets to use state funds to buy thousands of hogs from Georgia farmers, ship them to Chicago, and sell them there. He saved some hog farmers from bankruptcy, and the state only lost a few thousand dollars, but Talmadge had no legal authority to buy the hogs in the first place and was accused of stealing from the state. Talk of impeachment ran through the capital. Talmadge had always shown an uncanny ability to deflect criticism of his wrongdoing, but he left the legislative committee investigating the hog incident completely flummoxed when he testified, "Yeah, I stole, but I stole for farmers like you." Talmadge supporters who had come to Atlanta to watch the hearing hollered their approval, and the threat of impeachment dissolved.

In 1932, Talmadge set his sights on being governor. Even with the Depression crushing people's lives, Talmadge preached the same old bromides but offered no real solutions to their problems. He was more showman than ever. Men planted in the crowds yelled out pre-arranged questions like, "Gene, did you steal?" The crowd went wild when he answered, "Yeah, I stole, but I stole for *you*!" Talmadge minions also pulled dirty tricks, once setting a car on fire at an opposition gathering so that everyone rushed off to watch the excitement. The candidate was left alone.

Talmadge won the governorship and was re-elected in 1934, but controversy came fast after that. Just days after the polls closed, he declared martial law, called up 4,000 National Guard troops, and arrested thousands of men and women protesting the miserable working conditions at Georgia's mills.[4] On another occasion when the State Treasurer and Comptroller General wouldn't do his bidding, Talmadge ordered the National Guard to physically remove both men from the Capitol. Unable to open the safe with the men gone, Talmadge had it dynamited open.

Talmadge couldn't succeed himself as governor, so he ran for the U.S. Senate in 1936 and again in 1938, losing both times. He was hammered for his tyrannical rule as governor and decried in the press for having ruled as a dictator. With foresight no one then appreciated, the press asked whether the next step would be Talmadge seizing ballot boxes.[5] The Speaker of the House compared him to Hitler.[6]

Talmage ran again for governor in 1940 and won in a campaign marked by brawls. He spoke favorably of Hitler while Panzers rolled across Europe. He even referred to himself as a "minor dictator," but it was Talmadge's actions at the University of Georgia that brought him problems. When there was the slightest hint that a university professor was insufficiently committed to segregation, Talmadge forced two members of the Board of Regents to resign, replaced them with his puppets, and the professor was fired. The university lost its accreditation because of Talmadge's interference, and largely because of that he was defeated for re-election in 1942 by Ellis Arnall, a liberal by the country's standards of the day.

Arnall was re-elected two years later but couldn't succeed himself in 1946, and Talmadge was ready to run for governor again. In what shouldn't have been a big surprise, Georgia's politics were on the verge of unprecedented change. For decades, African Americans had been excluded from politics because the Democratic Party only allowed whites to vote in its primaries. On March 6, 1946, the federal court declared Georgia's white primary illegal.[7] African-American voter registration drives sprung up across the state, but at the same time, the court's decision energized white racists who saw Blacks voting as an existential threat to their way of life. The white primary issue and race would define the gubernatorial election.

The script couldn't have been written any better to fit Talmadge, a flamboyant demagogue willing to do anything to win. The hardcore racists in Georgia were the same men and women who had been his loyal supporters for twenty years. They were the have-nots of society, people who were angry for reasons they didn't really understand, and blaming Black people was an easy answer. They were joined in this election by wealthy people and businessmen who liked Talmadge's opposition to taxes, his hostility to New Deal social programs, and his opposition to labor unions. Poor white millworkers were caught between their dislike of Talmadge's anti-union stance and their ingrained racism. Too often the latter trumped the former, and they voted for Talmadge against their own self-interest.

Talmadge crafted his angry rhetoric to fuel white fears and convince voters that he alone could protect them from the "Negro threat." As governor, Ellis Arnall had ordered the attorney general to investigate the Klan and revoke its state charter so Georgia wouldn't be "a center of intolerance."[8] Talmadge, by comparison, sought Klan votes. His overt, vitriolic racism contributed to a resurgence of the Klan in 1946, and he promised he would have the legislature enact new laws to preserve the white primary and ensure that no Black person would ever cast a vote in Georgia again. It wasn't enough, though, for Talmadge to stop Black voters in future elections. To win the governor's race, he needed to stop African Americans from voting *now*. Any Black votes cast would go to James Carmichael, a liberal candidate in the mold of Ellis Arnall. As Talmadge said, "If I get a Negro vote it'll be an accident."[9]

To stop African Americans from voting, Talmadge ignored the law without a second thought. His thugs intimidated Blacks who tried to register, and his racist speeches incited whites to challenge Black people when they tried to register, and when they did register, to knock them off the rolls. Talmadge falsely claimed that thousands of Black registrants in Savannah and Atlanta were convicted criminals, one of the many lies he spread to inflame whites. It worked as intended. Angry whites took the cue and challenged Black voters as supposed criminals without a shred of evidence. In many counties, the fear of reprisals and physical violence was enough to keep Black people away from the voter registration office in the county courthouse. As Black people often said in 1946 and for many years afterwards, "nothing good ever happens to a Black man at the courthouse." Voter suppression continued right through election day as white men gathered at some polls to intimidate Black voters.[10] In the end, Talmadge stopped tens of thousands of African Americans who tried to vote; many thousands more never tried to register because of fear.

While Talmadge frightened white voters and played on the two centuries of racism that poisoned Georgia, many whites detested him and his extreme brand of racism. A majority of the newspapers across the state editorialized against him. The words of the *Atlanta Constitution* were hardly unique:

> Eugene Talmadge has run this race on a platform of bias and bigotry. He has constantly defied the Supreme Court of the United States and recommended action in open conflict with the law. He has preached hate and animosity. He has appealed to prejudice and inflamed passion. Instead of learning his lesson in 1942, he has come back in 1946 to redouble his venom, to redouble his duplicity, to reach heights of viciousness of which not even he had previously been thought capable.[11]

When the votes were finally tallied on July 17, 1946, Talmadge's attacks on Black voters had worked. Carmichael came in first in the popular vote, but the county unit system did what it was supposed to do—conservative, racist rural voters gave Talmadge a majority of the county unit votes and the Democratic nomination. Had tens of thousands of African Americans not been prevented from voting, Carmichael would have won the county unit vote as well as the popular vote and become governor.

Not only were many Georgians, both Black and white, appalled at Talmadge's nomination, national sentiment was equally negative. Even newspapers in conservative cities like Fredericksburg, Virginia, wrote that Talmadge's win had "all the earmarks of a Hitlerian victory."[12] The *Atlanta Daily World* was dismayed that the election revealed "to what extent the passion of racial prejudice can be inflamed."[13] Regardless, there being no Republican candidate, Talmadge's winning the Democratic nomination was as good as being elected governor—or so it seemed.

Talmadge was only sixty-one, but on the night of the primary election he felt much older. He had driven himself relentlessly during the campaign and was paying the price for years of hard drinking. He suffered from cirrhosis and a bleeding stomach and was exhausted. Uncharacteristically, he took a long trip after the election to relax and regain his strength, ending up in Florida to rest. Less than a week before returning to Georgia for the Democratic convention on October 9, however, he was rushed to a Jacksonville hospital at 2 a.m. in shock. While Talmadge had not looked well for months, this was the first time people close to him realized just how sick he was.

The person closest to Gene Talmadge was his thirty-three-year-old son, Herman, who had a law degree from Georgia. Herman had been a part of his father's campaigns since he was a child and managed the campaigns in 1938 and 1940. He was off with the Navy during World War II but was back in Georgia in 1945 and once again deep in family politics. Herman was Gene's campaign manager for the 1946 election and flew to Jacksonville immediately when his father was hospitalized. Gene looked much better after receiving blood transfusions, but his apparent improvement was deceptive.

The general election was on November 5, only four weeks off, but equally important was the date two months later, January 13, 1947, when the General Assembly would go into session. It was not until then that the new governor would be sworn into office. Three months could be a very long time for someone as sick as Gene Talmadge, but the possibility of Gene's death and what that meant for the governorship were not subjects that were talked about. To outsiders, Gene was presented as healthy and recovering. In the tight inner circle, Herman was the only person who might have moved people to grapple with the political consequences if Gene were to die, but it was too disheartening for him to do that.

Then, the course of history was changed by Gibson Ezell, a man of no particular significance in the politics of Georgia or the election of 1946, other than being a personal friend of Herman's and a longtime supporter of Gene Talmadge. Ezell was a school superintendent and the owner of a small store as well as a political junkie. He was the first person to do what others should have done already—he looked at the law to see what would happen if Gene died. The general election was soon, and dead or alive Gene would come in first as the only candidate on the ballot, so the question for Ezell was, "What happens if Gene doesn't make it to January when he is supposed to be sworn in?"

Georgians had just ratified an entirely new state constitution, and it was obvious the drafters never thought of this problem. The answer wasn't at all clear, and there was no precedent for how to deal with a situation in which a winning candidate died before being sworn in. The constitution provided that election returns for governor were to be opened and counted in the presence of the General Assembly when it convened in January, and the candidate with a majority of the votes would be elected governor. But if no one had a majority, "then from the two persons having the highest number of votes, who shall be in life [when the ballots are opened], the *General Assembly shall immediately elect a governor*." Ezell figured that Talmadge supporters controlled a majority of the legislators who would elect the next governor if Gene didn't survive. But for that to work, they would need a backup candidate they controlled to win enough votes in the general election to be one of the "two persons [in life] having the highest number of votes."

There was barely a week left before the general election when Ezell met with Herman to explain his idea.[14] Herman was convinced and immediately talked to several other lawyers to get their thoughts. They all agreed both as to what the constitution meant and the simple solution to the problem—get write-in votes for a candidate who could step in if Gene died and be selected by the legislature. The obvious choice as the write-in candidate was Herman. His name alone would carry many of the legislators. Herman called a few friends to get people to write in his name while keeping the plan as quiet as possible. If word got out that Gene was as sick as he was or that a backup write-in campaign was underway, there would be nothing to stop others from doing the same thing, and then there would be a race to get the most write-in votes.

Gene was in and out of the hospital, improving then relapsing, through the rest of November and into December. It was often said that everyone in Georgia was praying for Gene—half that he would recover and half that he would die. The latter half got their wish on December 21, 1946, when Gene died. According to the backup plan, the General Assembly would elect Herman governor in a few weeks, but the politics and the law got murky fast.

For one thing, Georgia's new constitution provided for a lieutenant governor for the first time. M. E. Thompson had won the democratic nomination and was unopposed on the November ballot for the new office. Had Gene Talmadge survived until he was sworn in and then died the next day, Thompson would have become governor. Thompson claimed he should become governor in this situation, too. The incumbent governor, Ellis Arnall, claimed that he should continue as governor because the law also provided that the incumbent governor would serve until the "election" of a "qualified" successor. Talmadge wasn't "qualified" by virtue of his death, and no one else had been elected governor, Arnall argued. Attorney General Eugene Cook issued an official opinion that agreed with Arnall, which didn't surprise anyone since Arnold had appointed Cook to be attorney general the year before.

On the first day of the new legislative session, January 13, 1947, the capital was more madhouse than a civilized assembly. Herman had called for Talmadge supporters to come to Atlanta to keep the pressure on the legislators as they decided who would be governor, and 10,000 men responded, many inebriated and some armed "just in case." The capitol building itself was packed with a noisy mob that filled the House gallery and forced its way onto the House floor where the members of both the House and Senate were trying to meet in a joint session.

The House elected Fred Hand, a Talmadge backer, as speaker, and Herman immediately took over Hand's spacious office suite as his base of operations. Thompson did the same on the Senate side. William Dean, a Thompson backer, was elected President of the Senate, and Thompson took over his office.

Time and again, Dean, who presided over the joint session, tried to clear the public from the House floor, but there was such bedlam that it wasn't until the afternoon of the next day that vote canvassing could begin. The returns from the counties had been sent to the secretary of state after the general election in two separate envelopes, one containing the returns for governor and the other the returns for lieutenant governor and other constitutional offices. Strategically, the order in which the returns would be published and acted upon took on tremendous importance.

There was no question that M. E. Thompson would be lieutenant governor. There was a good argument that that office should be addressed first since it was uncontroversial, but the consequences of doing so would be enormous. If Thompson were lieutenant governor, then Ellis Arnold—who by law held the office *until* he was succeeded—would resign and the vacancy would be automatically filled by Thompson. As a political and practical matter, that would put the Talmage faction in a much more difficult position. Voting Herman to be the governor would then require ousting Thompson and returning him to the position of lieutenant governor. As a matter of perception, that would look a lot like a coup and meet with more outrage than Talmadge already faced. To avoid that quagmire, the Talmage faction in the General Assembly needed to name Herman governor before Thompson became lieutenant governor.

Herman's legislative leader was J. Robert Elliott, a lawyer who had been away during World War II but was intimately familiar with the politics of the House since he had been elected to the legislature for the first time in 1936 when he was only twenty-seven years old. He had been re-elected in 1946 after he returned from the Navy and was a strong supporter of both Talmadges. Elliott introduced a resolution to establish a committee of tellers, composed of legislators, to canvass the returns for all nine constitutional offices. To maximize Talmadge's leverage, the resolution prohibited the tellers from even publishing the returns for any office other than governor until a governor was chosen *and* took office.

Before Elliott's resolution was voted on, a critical moment in the struggle for strategic advantage came when anti-Talmadge legislators offered an amendment that all the returns be reported and published at the same time and deleted the requirement that the governor be inaugurated before any other office was determined. They hoped they could get more support that way and Thompson could still be declared lieutenant governor first. The pressure over the vote on the amendment was unlike anything the legislators had experienced. It was correctly seen as a litmus test on Talmadge's support. In the end, it was defeated by the narrowest of margins, 128 to 126, and with that, Thompson's best strategic card was gone.

However, even though the procedure was now settled, the ultimate question still remained—who the General Assembly would elect as governor, or might the legislators punt the whole question to a special election, a solution preferred by many of them. Most people had assumed that Herman would have the most write-in votes ever since he had publicly acknowledged the write-in campaign after his father died. But the legislators and the Talmadge crowd who filled the capital were shocked when the envelopes with the counties' write-in votes were first opened. Herman was neither first nor second. He was third, which would make him ineligible to be selected as governor. James Carmichael received 669 votes, a man named Dewitt Bowers received 637 votes, and Herman received only 617 votes. While the committee of tellers didn't formally "report" those returns, word spread fast, and pandemonium broke out among the disappointed Talmage supporters and surprised legislators.

That Carmichael got the write-in votes he did should not have been a surprise. He had beaten Gene Talmadge in the popular vote in the July primary, and his supporters were so distraught at Gene's election that some write-in protest vote was inevitable. Bowers was more of a surprise, except for the fact that he had gotten write-in votes in previous elections by asking friends and neighbors to write him in as a lark, the same thing he did in 1946.

What happened next is one of the most brazen election heists in American history. According to Talmadge legislators, a consolidated return for fifty-eight additional votes for Herman were conveniently "found" after midnight in the "wrong" envelope from Telfair County. The fifty-eight additional votes were just enough to put Herman in first place with 675 votes, six more than Carmichael, and make Herman eligible to be picked as governor. It was that revised total that the teller committee reported to the General Assembly as the true vote.

What only a very few legislators knew at the time was that the reported returns were anything but "true." The additional fifty-eight votes were entirely fraudulent. No one ever confessed to the crime, but the facts that quickly became known proved to a certainty that the votes were fraudulent.[15]

At the outset, it made no sense that *some* gubernatorial returns from Telfair County were in the envelope containing the returns for the *other* offices since other gubernatorial returns from Telfair were in the correct envelope. Furthermore, after the magic fifty-eight votes were added, Herman had seventy-seven write-in votes from Telfair County and forty-eight from the Helena precinct alone, but at the time of the general election the county had reported to the local newspaper that Herman had received no votes in the Helena precinct. No one could explain this disparity nor could they explain how more votes were reported from the county than the number of people who voted. The chairman of the county election managers remembered that Herman had gotten some write-in votes, but he was "doggoned if I could remember him having as many as 65."[16]

More damning proof of the Telfair County fraud was a fictitious list of thirty-four voters who supposedly cast a ballot in the Helena precinct—*all of them voting in alphabetical order*. The alphabetical names of supposed voters all began only with the letters A through K. None started with L or later letters of the alphabet. What had happened was obvious. The Talmadge man who created the fraudulent votes took the list of registered voters that is prepared, in alphabetical order, before an election. It is that list that the precinct manager uses to check to see if a voter is registered. When someone votes, they are checked off that list. The Talmadge rogue went down that list of names and copied, in order, those who had *not* voted. Possibly because he was so pressed for time, he didn't think how incriminating his list would be since it was inconceivable that dozens of voters just happened to arrive at the poll and voted in alphabetical order. To top off the proof of fraud, some of the people who were added had died long before the election, a number did not exist at all, others had moved away and no longer voted in Telfair County, and others denied voting in the election.

The Secretary of State, Ben Fortson, was forty-two years old and had custody of both sets of envelopes from the counties until he turned them over to the legislature on January 14. Fortson was still Georgia's secretary of state thirty years later, and I knew him because of election cases I was handling in the 1970s. One day we talked about the infamous 1946 election, and Fortson shared with me his view of how the fake returns came about. When the Talmadge people realized Herman was falling short, they knew they could get fraudulent votes from Telfair County, Gene's home, but they needed a little time because Telfair County was over 100 miles away. According to Fortson, Talmadge men started fires in the Capitol and shot off their pistols to slow the count repeatedly until it dragged into the early hours of January 15. He never saw the falsified returns until after they had been "found" but believed they had to have been added during the turmoil.

As Fortson saw what was happening, he worried about who Herman might appoint to state offices if he seized the governorship. There was ample reason for his concern since Gene and Herman, together, had named a long list of Klan members as delegates to the Democratic Party convention in October.

Talmadge would need the official state seal to make appointment certificates legal, but Fortson, as secretary of state, was the custodian of that seal. Fortson had been paralyzed and in a wheelchair because of an auto accident since he was twenty-four years old, and during the chaos of January 14 and 15, he put the state seal under the seat of his wheelchair so Talmadge's people couldn't find it. He laughed when he told me he gave Talmadge an old Georgia colonial seal instead, which had no legal effect.

Had the vote fraud been known to all of the legislators in the early morning hours of January 15, Herman wouldn't have been named governor. But with only a very few legislators in Talmadge's inner circle knowing the truth, the climax of the governor's race would finally be decided by the raw political power of the Talmadge and anti-Talmadge factions in the legislature.

Talmadge, Carmichael, and Thompson had all been trying to muster a majority even before Gene Talmadge's death. Some legislators said they had been offered bribes. Now, with the fraudulent write-in vote announced, the weeks of jockeying and lobbying were about to end. Elliott introduced a resolution declaring that, given Gene's death, the constitution required the General Assembly to elect a governor from the top two remining candidates who were "in life" and willing to serve.

Anti-Talmadge legislators introduced a counter-resolution that the constitution did not allow the legislature to choose a governor since there had been a "majority winner" in the general election. Instead, the legislature could only provide for a special election to fill the office. The competing resolutions were the final showdown between the factions in the legislature, and the anti-Talmadge motion failed by a vote of 132 to 118. Elliott's motion then passed, and he nominated Herman as governor. With Carmichael then believing he couldn't win the legislative vote, he declined to compete, and Herman was elected governor with 161 affirmative votes and eighty-seven legislators voting "present" in protest.

Talmadge was sworn in immediately and went straight to the governor's office on the first floor of the Capitol accompanied by a raucous crowd of supporters and a phalanx of twenty-five legislators who had been directed by the General Assembly to "install the newly elected Governor in the Governor's office in the capitol building." Arnall was inside the governor's office with the front door to the reception area locked. Some of Talmadge's mob broke the door down and were about to grab Arnall and throw him out when Talmadge interceded. As Talmadge recalled the scene years later, there were about "10,000 people in the capitol that night, most of them my friends, some of them had been drinking, some of them armed, and it was a right volatile situation."[17] The two gubernatorial claimants faced off like roosters. Talmadge demanded of Arnall that he leave, asking, "Do you defy the General Assembly?" Arnall refused and replied that Talmadge was just a "pretender" to the office.

Talmadge and Thompson supporters got into brawls, but surprisingly no one was shot. The Georgia National Guard, which had been called up for the war, had been deactivated and was in Georgia and loyal to Talmadge. He ordered the Guard to escort Arnall to his home in Newnan, about forty miles from the Capitol, and be sure that "no harm befall him." Talmadge also directed the Guard to come right back and change the locks on the governor's office. Talmadge was concerned enough about possible violence after the ruckus at the Capitol that he took to carrying a .38 pistol for some time.

People were worried about a military confrontation since both Talmadge and Arnall controlled a *de facto* army. Opposing Talmadge's National Guard was the Georgia State Guard that was loyal to Arnall. Talmadge ordered the State Guard disbanded, saying it was no longer needed since the National Guard back from the war, but Arnall said Talmadge's order was meaningless since Talmadge wasn't the real governor. The general in command of the nearby Fifth Wing of the International Guard was on alert in case he was needed to keep peace between the competing armies.[18]

Locked out of the governor's office, Arnall set up a desk in the Capitol rotunda and carried on what business of the state he could from there. That gave rise to more rumors that Talmadge would use the National Guard to evict

Arnall from the Capitol,[19] but Arnall left voluntarily after an enormous firecracker was exploded behind him. From his Atlanta law office, he tried to carry out the duties of governor the best he could as "The Three Governor Dispute" raged on.

While Talmadge tried to solidify his control over the state government, anti-Talmadge demonstrators protested his seizure of power. Arnall condemned him as a demagogue and storm trooper, and the Atlanta newspapers were scalding:

> The people of Georgia are awakening that the enemies of freedom and constitutional government are now on the retreat and are behind their barred doors, guarded by goons, thugs and storm troopers, scalawags and hirelings. This fight in Georgia is a fight for all America. This is a deliberate experiment of whether Nazi methods . . . can be used to seize the Government by force. That was the formula in Italy and Germany. The formula is the same—the political trickery, the use of carefully calculated force backed by an irresponsible and half-drunken mob, the defiance of the courts and public opinion.[20]

Talmadge taunted the protestors, saying he could have 25,000 of his supporters in Atlanta overnight if need be.

On January 18, Thompson got into the action by taking the oath of office for lieutenant governor. Arnall promptly resigned his claim to the governorship and said that Thompson, as the duly elected lieutenant governor, was automatically the acting governor. Attorney General Cook again issued a ruling that agreed with Arnall.

The fight between the Talmadge and anti-Talmadge factions sharpened and temperatures continued to rise. The competing governors made dual appointments to state offices, but no one knew who had authority to act. The attorney general refused to approve a bond that was necessary for banks to issue state funds because the bond was made payable to "Governor Talmadge."

When the bond was reissued to "The Governor," Cook was satisfied and the state could finally pay its bills.

To Georgia's citizens, the controversy was catastrophic. Talmadge supporters felt they had won but were under siege, and the more numerous anti-Talmadge faction thought their government had been seized in a coup d'état. Outside of Georgia, the state's dysfunctional politics were decried as a failure of democracy and ridiculed by comedians and journalists.[21]

The question of who was the rightful governor reached the Georgia Supreme Court very quickly, but before the court ruled, the *Atlanta Journal* published an investigation by a young reporter, C. E. Gregory, that was devastating for Talmadge. It showed in exacting detail that the Telfair County votes that brought Herman from third place to first were fraudulent.[22] What many people thought had happened was now clearly proved, and Gregory's work received a Pulitzer Prize. Whatever chance Talmadge might have had in court before that bombshell was now gone.

The court issued its decision just two weeks after the article and ruled that Arnall had been entitled to remain as governor after Gene Talmadge died. Because Arnall had agreed to resign his office, Lieutenant Governor Thompson was now the rightful governor. The Georgia Supreme Court also ruled that Thompson would serve as governor only until the next general election in November 1948. Gubernatorial terms had been extended to four years by Georgia's new 1945 Constitution, but Thompson would only serve until someone was elected to serve out the remaining two years of the original term.

Herman Talmadge's corrupt seizure of the governor's office was stopped, and the voters would have another chance to elect a governor soon. That would assuage some of the anger Talmadge voters felt over losing their governor.

In the run-up to the court's decision, no one was sure what Talmadge would do if the court ruled against him, but he vacated the governor's office the same day. Laws passed by the legislature and signed by Talmadge became void unless signed again by Thompson. The one law that everyone was concerned about was the bill that Talmadge had pushed through the General Assembly to maintain the white primary. When Thompson became governor, he vetoed Talmadge's white primary bill, and that was the end of white primaries in Georgia.

Eugene Talmadge gave Georgia a conflagration of bigotry and corruption that had long seemed nothing more than a distant aberration in the nation's history, but that sordid fiasco now seems more relevant than most Americans would have imagined a few years ago. A mob descended on the U.S. Capitol on January 6, 2021, to stop the counting of electoral votes and install as president the losing candidate. False claims of illegal voting are proclaimed from the highest offices. Voter suppression is pursued by private groups, by state and federal legislatures, and by government agencies.

There is much to learn from the Talmadge elections and Talmadge campaigns. They are more than "just history" and hold insights about politicians and elections that are ignored at our peril.

3

Lyndon Johnson—Two Stolen Elections on the Way to the Presidency

Lyndon Johnson was born on a small farm on the Pedernales River in the Texas Hill Country and spent most of his childhood a few miles from there in Johnson City, but "city" is a misnomer by any standard. Johnson City was the county seat of Blanco County, but its population was a meager 400 when Johnson graduated from the local high school. The Texas Hill Country was poor. Settlers had degraded the land by overgrazing, and the loss of prairie grass had caused erosion that washed away the already thin soil. Like many people there, Lyndon's father, Sam Ealy Johnson, Jr., struggled financially, and Lyndon was driven to escape the poverty of his surroundings from an early age. Sam Johnson served several terms in the Texas House of Representatives, and Lyndon learned the ways of the legislature going with his father to Austin when he was still a boy.

Johnson had to borrow $27 in 1927 to enroll at the Southwest Texas Teachers College where he supported himself working as a janitor and helping the college president. After graduating, he was teaching at a Houston high school when he received a call from Richard Kleberg that changed his life. Kleberg was one of the richest men in Texas and the scion of the family that owned the fabulous King Ranch, which was bigger than the state of Rhode Island and ran over 200 miles from the Hill Country to the southern border of Texas. Kleberg had just won a special election to fill a vacancy in the 14th Congressional District, and he wanted Johnson to serve as his congressional administrative secretary. Johnson was ecstatic. It was his dream job. Even better, Kleberg had little interest in the duties of a congressman, which meant Johnson would have tremendous responsibility and little supervision.

Johnson knew next to nothing about the operations of the federal government when he arrived in Washington, but he worked day and night to learn and soon functioned like a de facto congressman because of Kleberg's indifference to the office. Everyone agreed Johnson was "a prodigious worker, incredible energy—mental and physical."[1] He mastered the art of constituent service and became a master of federal agencies. He had a unique ability to cajole and charm—or threaten when necessary—to get what he wanted for Kleberg's constituents. He wasn't above palming himself off as the congressman if need be to get what he wanted.

The "Little Congress" was an informal group of congressional aides that Johnson saw as a way to connect with colleagues and learn more about the ins and outs of the Hill. But in typical Johnson fashion, he wasn't content being a mere member; he wanted to be the Little Congress' Speaker. The Speaker was usually determined by seniority, but Johnson had no time to wait for that. He encouraged new groups of congressional employees who had not been active in the organization to join, and they voted Johnson in as Speaker. Johnson used his new position to cultivate congressmen, newspapermen, and lobbyists, and his expanding network of friends soon included aides to President Roosevelt and fellow Texans like Vice President John Nance Garner and Congressman Sam Rayburn.

Johnson left Washington in 1935 to run the Texas office of the National Youth Administration, a New Deal agency. The work required him to travel throughout Texas to find financial sponsors for NYA construction projects.

Within six months, 18,000 young Texans were working on public projects, men who would be grateful to Johnson in future elections.

Two years later, the incumbent congressman in the 10th Congressional District, James Buchanan, died, which meant there would be a special election to fill the vacancy. Johnson didn't think twice. The 10th district included the Texas Hill Country and the state capital of Austin, where he now lived, and if Johnson was ever going to succeed in politics, this was his opportunity. But he wasn't very well known by the district's voters. The long list of constituents who were grateful to him were all in Kleberg's 14th Congressional District. Moreover, at twenty-eight years old, Johnson was just three years over the constitutional minimum and younger than all but two current members of Congress.

If Texas politicos had been polled about the likely successor to Buchanan, Johnson would have been far down the list, but they would not have understood the energy Johnson would bring to the race, nor would they have understood Johnson's ability to parlay the contacts he had made. One of those was Alvin Wirtz, an Austin lawyer, past President *pro tem* of the Texas Senate, and a formidable lobbyist for Texas oil and gas interests. Wirtz knew politics as well as anyone, he could raise large sums of money for a candidate, and most importantly, he loved Lyndon Johnson like a son. He was the architect of Johnson's campaign strategy as well as an entrée to the state's moneyed political contributors.

The 10th district was vast—8,000 square miles, bigger than some eastern states—and sparsely populated except for Austin. There were only six weeks from Buchanan's death to the April 10 special election, and Johnson raised and spent between $75,000 and $100,000,[2] an extraordinary sum for the time that dwarfed what other candidates spent. Johnson outworked every other candidate as he drove around the enormous district and spoke wherever he could, seven days a week. Never a good public speaker, Johnson was unparalleled in his ability to connect to individuals when he walked through a crowd and spoke to them one-on-one. He was engaging, persuasive, and it was the rare person who didn't commit to "help" Johnson after they got the personal treatment.

When the short but intense campaign was near its end, Johnson was in such pain from appendicitis that he couldn't stand without help, but he insisted on shaking voters' hands until he was finally rushed off for an emergency appendectomy. When the polls closed and the votes were totaled, Johnson had less than 30 percent but that was substantially more than anyone else. Since there was no majority vote requirement in the special election, Johnson was now a congressman.

Johnson's next chance to climb the political ladder came four years later when eighty-seven-year-old Texas Senator Morris Sheppherd died in April 1941. A special election to fill the vacancy would be held on Saturday, June 28, just weeks away. The minute Johnson heard the news he was off and running. Like the other special elections, there would be no primary and no runoff even if no one won a majority.

Johnson's earlier race in the 10th District was grueling because of the immensity of the district, but a statewide race in Texas was a whole different matter. Texas was not just the biggest state in the union at the time; it was *twenty-five times bigger* than nearly every state in New England. To cover Texas, a candidate had to travel 800 miles north to south and 800 miles east to west, and the population was still predominantly rural. Texas also had 254 counties, each with its own political leader and, in some counties, local bosses who controlled the vote.

Johnson's weakness in his first congressional race—lack of name recognition—would be his weakness again multiplied severalfold running statewide. Because the qualifying fee to run was only one dollar, the race drew twenty-five candidates, but only a few were even slightly serious. Of those, several had much greater name recognition than Johnson, including the young Texas Attorney General, Gerald Mann. Mann had a reputation as a smart, able reformer, uncompromised by special interests, and he was very popular.

Congressman Martin Dies, Jr, was the chairman of the notorious House Committee on Un-American Activities (HUAC), which Congress established in 1938. Ostensibly created to investigate Nazis and similar groups that posed a danger to the United States as fascism spread in Europe, Dies used the committee more to harass labor unions and New Deal agencies. President Roosevelt was aghast at the thought of Dies becoming a senator. Dies was a Democrat in name, but Johnson could attack his extreme conservatism and opposition to the New Deal in a state that Roosevelt had won overwhelmingly.

The incumbent Texas Governor, W. Lee (Pappy) O'Daniel, had extremely high visibility and was revered by much of the electorate. He was the one possible candidate that Johnson was afraid could beat him. When O'Daniel said he wasn't running, Johnson felt he had a winning path to the Senate even though initial polls showed him with only 5 percent of the vote. Johnson expected help from Roosevelt who liked Johnson and was grateful for the strong support he got from the young congressman on New Deal legislation.

Running a Texas campaign required money, lots of money, and there Johnson had an advantage. The kinds of connections he had when he ran for Congress in 1937 had been nurtured, often through his help as a congressman who "delivered the goods" to Texas business interests. Johnson's most loyal financial support came from Herman Brown, founder of Brown & Root, an extremely successful Texas contracting firm. Brown had a special affinity for Johnson and vice versa because they had both started out poor and craved success from an early age.

Money was necessary to fund campaign staff who could cover the state; to buy advertisements in the hundreds of local newspapers that were the only source of news for many people; and to buy as much radio time as possible. All this was necessary so that voters would know the name Lyndon Johnson when they went to vote. Johnson also needed to spend money to be sure voters knew who Dies really was, an anti-Roosevelt, anti-New Deal reactionary.

But money was necessary in Texas for other reasons. In some counties, money had to be paid to men who could turn out the vote because that required a lot of footwork going door to door to talk to voters and ensure they voted on election day. The people who did that work needed to be paid. In some counties, money could be paid to someone solely for his endorsement and that alone would carry votes.

That wasn't all that money could buy in some Texas counties, however. In some places money had a more pernicious power, outright vote buying on a big, Texas-sized scale. In a close election, crooked votes could make a difference. Sometimes, a corrupt election judge would even switch the winner of a county's votes after the polls closed, not to change the outcome of the election but just to have his county shown as supporting the winner so he might reap some benefits for supposedly "delivering the vote."

One of the most infamous men in local Texas politics was George Parr, whose father, Archie Parr, had controlled the votes in the Valley counties on the Mexican border since 1911. Whoever Parr supported got those votes. "When the returns came in [they were] always lopsided for one candidate down in that area of the state."[3] But even with Parr, it wasn't clear that he was always paid to deliver the vote. He had made a lot of money and hardly needed an election payoff.[4] Parr's influence over voters came from his personal relationships with the near-destitute Mexican-American population. He routinely advanced or outright gave money to people for medical care they couldn't afford, and people revered him for what he did for them.

In a few counties, the vote bosses were the same men who paid impoverished Mexican Americans the pittance they received for back-breaking work. While their wages were next to nothing, they were all that kept a man's family from starvation, and if the boss told a man how to vote, that's how he voted. The worst of the bosses were backed by gun-toting thugs who made sure people voted on election day. Those bosses had no compunction about selling their employees' votes.

As the election neared, Johnson felt more and more confident. At the end of May, the polls showed he was still behind Mann, but the gap was much less than it had been. Then, suddenly, without any warning, the election was turned upside down. Governor Pappy O'Daniel jumped into the race with only a month to go. Johnson was so depressed he spent almost two weeks in a hospital, his campaign surrogates saying he was resting from the intense campaign schedule, which was partly true. Remarkably, when he emerged from the hospital, he showed no sign of weakness, no weariness, and no fear. It was a revived, fully energized Lyndon Johnson, ready to do battle.

Pappy O'Daniel provides one of the country's strangest political stories, his path to office the opposite of Johnson's. He was a showman who knew nothing about public policy or government, had never been involved in anything political before he ran for governor in 1938, and was so uninterested in politics he had never even voted. O'Daniel had been a flour salesman who also worked as a radio announcer and showed a genius—and a mesmerizing voice—for spinning corny country stories and advice about life. After a while, half the housewives in Texas were tuning in everyday to listen to him. As a reporter wrote at the time: "At twelve-thirty sharp each day, a fifteen-minute silence reigned in the state of Texas, broken only by mountain music, and the dulcet voice of W. Lee O'Daniel."[5]

Johnson's campaign was forced to do an immediate about face when O'Daniel jumped into the race. Johnson had been running a dignified campaign to appear like a senator, but that was over. Now he was running against a vaudeville showman. Johnson did have one big advantage, however—money. It was so limitless that the campaign decided to give it away to people who came to hear him! Everyone who came to a rally got a lottery ticket for a chance to win Defense Bonds, and crowds that had been a few hundred swelled to a few thousand. Johnson drew record crowds of more than 25,000 in Austin and Dallas and reporters wrote of his "spectacular campaign."[6]

With only a few weeks left before the election, O'Daniel had not been out campaigning because the legislature was still in session and, as governor, he couldn't leave Austin. Nearly all of the legislators disliked O'Daniel and were happy to help Johnson by staying in session to keep O'Daniel off the campaign trail. When the legislature finally adjourned *after* the election, it had become the longest session in Texas history.

Johnson also turned the tables on O'Daniel with a clever but very risky move. O'Daniel's strongest supporters were old people who believed he was trying to get the legislature to give them a pension. Johnson decided to heap praise on O'Daniel for his pension efforts and then get voters thinking, if O'Daniel went to the Senate, their state pensions were dead. The tactic worked. Rural voters who loved O'Daniel wrote him asking him to withdraw from the race!

On Saturday night with 96 percent of the vote counted, Johnson was ahead by over 5,000 votes. On Monday morning, the manager of the Texas Election Bureau, an arm of the *Dallas Morning News* that gathered early returns, announced that "near-final returns virtually assured" a Johnson victory and "only a miracle could give O'Daniel a chance to overcome the lead."[7] In fact, there was one way other than a miracle for O'Daniel to win—Texas election fraud.

John Connally, Johnson's campaign manager, was hard working, politically ambitious, and would be elected governor of Texas twenty years later. But now he was only twenty-four years old and had a lot to learn about the seamy side of Texas politics. Unfortunately for Lyndon Johnson, Connally learned at Johnson's expense. Counties that were pro-Johnson called Connally to tell him their vote totals and asked if they should report them to the Election Bureau right away. Connally thought the election was over and saw no reason to wait, so he told them to report their returns. That decision would cost Johnson the election.

Connally had violated a cardinal rule of Texas politics—never let the opposition know how many votes you have until *all* the votes have been returned to the state. If you report early, you're telling your opponent how many additional votes they need to "find" to win.

As soon as O'Daniel's supporters knew Johnson's lead, "late" election returns from East Texas began to chew away at Johnson's lead. Ironically, those votes for O'Daniel had not been purchased by people who liked O'Daniel. The exact opposite was the case. People and businesses who couldn't stand O'Daniel supported his bid for the Senate to get him out of the governor's office.

Lieutenant Governor Coke Stevenson wanted O'Daniel to win, of course, so he would become governor. On Sunday, Stevenson told O'Daniel he would win the final count even though he was 5,000 votes behind. What Stevenson knew was that local election officials in counties where Dies was strong had agreed to hold their returns and, if Dies was out of the running, flip the vote totals of the two candidates, Dies and O'Daniel.[8]

When he realized his blunder, Connally blamed himself for Johnson losing the election:

> Governor O'Daniel and his people knew exactly how many votes they had to have to take the lead. They kept changing the results, and our lead got smaller and smaller and smaller. Finally, on Wednesday afternoon, we wound up on the short side of the stick and lost the election by 1,311 votes. I am basically responsible for losing that 1941 campaign. We let them know exactly how many votes they had to have.[9]

Johnson was furious when he saw his victory evaporating, but it's likely he was as mad at himself as much as anyone. Johnson was a detail-focused candidate who should have foreseen what would happen. One thing was certain though. If Johnson were ever to run for the Senate again, no one was going to steal the election from him.

The 1941 special election was followed just months later by Pearl Harbor, and the U.S. was in the middle of World War II. Johnson was the first member of Congress to enter active service when he joined the Naval Reserve as a lieutenant commander. When the time to qualify for election came in 1942, he was undecided whether to run for Congress again or to run against O'Daniel for a full term in the Senate. In one of the strangest chapters of any political career, Johnson filled out forms to qualify for both offices and left them with John Connally when Johnson went to the South Pacific on war service. Before he left, he told Connally to talk to their political friends and then "you make up your mind which position you want to file me for."[10] Connally ultimately decided to file Johnson's papers to run for re-election to his congressional seat. Johnson didn't know which office he was running for until he was told later.

Johnson's next chance to reach the Senate came in 1948 when the seat he had lost in 1941 was up again, and O'Daniel declined to run for re-election. Since this was a regular election, not a special election to fill a vacancy, there would first be a Democratic primary on Saturday, July 24, and if no candidate won a majority of the votes, there would be a runoff between the top two candidates on Saturday, August 28. By running for the Senate, Johnson was giving up re-election to his congressional seat and was resolved to leave politics behind if he didn't win.

There was a total of eleven candidates in the primary, but only two were a concern—former Governor Coke Stevenson and George Peddy. Stevenson was extremely popular and much better known than Johnson, having just left the governor's office in January 1947. Peddy was a lawyer, a veteran of both world wars, and an ex-member of the state legislature who had run unsuccessfully for the U.S. Senate in 1922. The early polls showed Johnson far behind Stevenson. The only question in the press was whether Stevenson would win outright in the initial election or would need a runoff to secure the nomination. Peddy's candidacy probably helped Johnson because he would take conservative votes from Stevenson and might prevent him from winning a majority on July 24.

The campaign bore a lot of similarities to the 1941 race. Johnson again had a tremendous amount of money, though more was always needed. When the July election was over, Johnson had climbed a long way from the initial polls, but he still took only 33.7 percent of the vote to 39.7 percent for Stevenson.

There were five weeks until the runoff, and those five weeks stand as one of the most intense, hard-fought, and byzantine elections in the country's history. Several times, it looked like one candidate had won and would go to the Senate, only to see their positions reversed days later.

Johnson had a big organizational advantage. He had planned for a runoff all along while Stevenson assumed he would win a majority in the initial race and didn't plan for a runoff. Johnson had campaign representatives in all of Texas' 254 counties, and on election day, there was a Johnson representative at nearly every precinct to watch for cheating.[11] Stevenson had nothing like that.

Nowhere was the lack of organization in Stevenson's campaign more dramatic than in Kinney and Hansford counties, both of which had given Stevenson a solid majority in the initial contest. The local politicians in those counties assumed Stevenson would win the runoff so easily that they didn't bother to hold a runoff in their counties! The Stevenson campaign didn't even realize those counties had "dropped out" until after the election was over. While both counties had relatively small populations, Stevenson would have picked up hundreds more votes had the polls simply been opened.

Stevenson's campaign had another flaw, and Johnson knew how to exploit it. Stevenson was overly proud and rigid. When he was asked questions in a way he didn't like, he was dismissive of the questioner. At a press conference in Washington, Stevenson was confronted by reporters who were more aggressive than he was accustomed to in Texas, and one asked about his position on the Taft-Hartley Act, anti-union legislation that Congress had passed recently. Stevenson was angered not by the question but by the "impolite," insistent way it was asked, and he gave evasive answers just because the reporter irritated him.

Texas voters were mostly anti-union conservatives who favored Taft-Hartley, and when newspaper headlines accused Stevenson of "dodging" questions about the legislation, conservatives who supported him began to wonder—would Stevenson vote to weaken the law if he won the election? The

Johnson campaign capitalized on the newspaper stories and got the message in front of voters everywhere. They reprinted one of the articles, mailed it to voters, made speeches about it, and purchased radio time throughout the state to hammer home the line that Stevenson was dodging the issue. The attack worked. Stevenson lost voters, and business interests who had been funding his campaign stopped contributing.

Johnson had to go after Peddy's conservative voters to have any chance to win. Peddy was strongest in East Texas, and Johnson tried to connect with the crowds there by saying how much he admired Peddy and how they were close to each other on many issues (which they weren't), and then reminding the voters of Stevenson's failings.

Johnson had another big advantage over Stevenson—his wife, Lady Bird Johnson. Lady Bird had been very helpful to Johnson throughout his political career with advice and insight, as well as her family money that seeded his first race for Congress, but she was terrified at the thought of delivering speeches. To everyone's surprise, she put aside her anxiety and undertook a speaking tour of the state, especially to women's groups. People who heard her became enthusiastic Johnson voters.

When the polls closed on Saturday, August 28, Johnson's campaign wanted to ensure there was no repeat of the mistake they had made in 1941. They did the opposite and purposely *underreported* Johnson's votes to the Election Bureau. As Connally explained, "In 1948 I said, 'Underreport your votes. Do not tell them how many total votes you have, just say it's incomplete.'"[12] That gave Johnson some protection from the kind of fraud Stevenson was involved in for O'Daniel in 1941, but it also guaranteed there would be accusations against the Johnson campaign as post-election returns from his counties became more favorable. The Johnson campaign told as many as fifty counties to underreport their initial vote.[13]

As the returns came in, it was clear this election would be as close as 1941, and controversy, accusations, and counter-accusations of cheating exploded from both sides. The first returns came in from Houston, Dallas, and Fort Worth because they had begun using voting machines instead of paper ballots. That not only sped up the count but also reduced innocent mistakes that were inevitable with paper ballots. It also made cheating more difficult. In the early morning of the day after the election, Johnson was reported to be behind by 854 votes. The Stevenson campaign frantically called people in proStevenson counties and told them to hold off reporting until they knew Johnson's totals. Stevenson had been neck-deep in the O'Daniel election theft in 1941 and wanted to avoid Connally's mistake from that year.

By Monday, there were constant updates and additional returns, some favoring Stevenson, some favoring Johnson. In Johnson's case, that was primarily a result of counties correcting totals they had previously underreported intentionally. At the end of that day, the Texas Election Bureau had Stevenson ahead by a mere 119 votes.[14]

Amended and corrected returns continued to come in during the week, with Stevenson taking a lead of up to 300 votes on Thursday. Then, on Friday, September 3, corrected and updated returns came from several Valley counties favoring Johnson, but it was one county in particular—Jim Wells County—that caused an uproar that still reverberates today. The Jim Wells County Democratic Executive Committee met on Friday to certify the vote to the State Democratic Executive Committee. As the tally sheets were opened, twelve of the county's precincts were the same as had been preliminarily reported on election night, but one precinct—what became the infamous "Box 13"—reported 200 more Johnson votes than it had originally. The Jim Wells Democratic Executive Committee certified the total to the state committee, and with the additional votes from the Valley counties, including Box 13, Johnson was now the winner of the election by *eighty-seven votes of the nearly one million cast.*

Stevenson was livid and claimed the election had been stolen by vote fraud in the Valley counties. His accusations were met by equally vehement counter-accusations of fraud in counties that went heavily for Stevenson. As soon as possible, Stevenson went to Alice, the county seat of Jim Wells County, with a team of lawyers, three ex-FBI agents, and a retired Texas Ranger reputed to be the toughest and most intimidating lawman in Texas. They weren't given enough time to copy the Box 13 voter list, but during the time they were allowed they saw what looked like classic signs of fraud. The last 200 names appeared to be in alphabetical order, and Stevenson swore that a "7" and been overwritten on a tally sheet to look like a "9," creating an additional 200 votes and making the Box 13 total 965 instead of the original 765. Incredibly, the Box 13 voter list was never made available for a full examination.

Armed with his evidence, Stevenson was hoping to get the Jim Wells County Executive Committee to change its vote certification to the State Party, and the committee agreed to meet on Saturday, September 11, to consider the evidence. Johnson's victory would disappear if the county committee changed its certification. The national media had now descended on Texas, and tension in the two campaigns and throughout the state was at a breaking point.

The State Democratic Party had the ultimate authority to designate its Senate nominee for the general election ballot, and the State Party was having its annual convention in Fort Worth on Monday, September 13. Reports of the votes from the 254 county executive committees would first be reviewed by the State Canvassing Subcommittee, then the subcommittee would report its recommendation to the State Democratic Executive Committee.

Under tremendous pressure to stop the Jim Wells County Committee from reversing its original decision, Johnson's lawyers filed a lawsuit on Friday, September 10, alleging that it would be illegal to change the county's certification at that point. A judge in Austin issued an order stopping the committee from doing anything until a full hearing on Monday in Alice. The Jim Wells County Committee had just begun to consider changing its vote certification on Saturday morning when telegrams were delivered announcing the court's order. The meeting was over until Monday.

The Monday court hearing in Alice was now on the same schedule as the Democratic Convention, and it was an all-out race between Stevenson and Johnson. If the restraining order was lifted on Monday in time to allow the county committee to revise its report, Stevenson would be the next senator. But if Johnson could get the State Executive Committee to act before the county committee, he should end up as the party's nominee. That Friday and Saturday witnessed the most intense politicking, arm twisting, and threats ever experienced in the wild history of Texas politics. Every big political actor in the state was drawn in, and, just as important, many of the state's wealthiest businessmen were in the fray, some on their own initiative, others dragged in on behalf of one candidate or the other to lobby the executive committee. Some committee members who hadn't planned on attending the convention had been told they had no choice; they needed to come to Fort Worth to vote.

The Canvassing Subcommittee that met on Monday morning had seven members: two representing Stevenson, two representing Johnson, and three who were neutral. The arguments by the candidates' representatives were heated; Stevenson's attorney used the word fraud as often as possible. Johnson's attorney threw similar charges at Stevenson and made the simple argument that, under Texas law, the existing county certification had to be honored. In the midst of the donnybrook, news came from Jim Wells County. When Stevenson's lawyer learned that the Canvassing Subcommittee was considering Jim Wells County, he told the judge that there was no longer any need for the hearing, hoping the judge would dissolve the restraining order. But instead, the judge left the injunction in place until a full trial took place.[15]

While that was good news for Johnson, he was about to get very bad news from the subcommittee. Johnson's attorneys had told him that the subcommittee was legally bound to accept the unamended certification from Jim Wells County. That may have been correct legally, but the subcommittee wasn't buying it. One of the members moved that all but the Jim Wells returns be certified, which would make Stevenson the winner. In a dreadful shock to

Johnson's lawyers, the subcommittee voted four to three in favor of the Stevenson motion. The full executive committee was going to meet in two hours, and Johnson now faced an uphill battle he never expected. He had to convince a majority of the executive committee members to reject the report and recommendation of its own subcommittee.

To the very last minute when the executive committee was polled, no one knew what the result would be. Some committee members had promised *both* sides they would vote for them. When the polling began, the room was teeming with anxiety, hostility, and raw fear. Johnson initially fell far behind, but then the vote went in his favor, and he eked out a win by a single vote, twenty-nine to twenty-eight. But as with everything else in this election, nothing was ever really over when it seemed to be. A committee member now stood and announced that she wished to change her vote from Johnson to merely reflect that she was "present" because she thought the whole matter should be decided by a court.[16] That threw the vote into a tie, and shouts of shock, anger, and celebration rocked the building.

With the vote tied, the executive committee had to be polled all over again. What had been unbearable tension worsened, and the likely outcome was still completely unknown. As the second polling was underway, Connally noticed that one executive committee member who had committed to vote for Johnson, Charlie Gibson, was not in the room, though Connally had seen him in the building. Connally rushed out and found him in the bathroom, probably trying to avoid voting, then dragged him into the assembly room where he yelled out his vote for Johnson as he came through the door, breaking the tie and giving Johnson the win by a single vote, twenty-nine to twenty-eight.[17] The chairman immediately gaveled the matter concluded so no one else could change their vote, and the next day the full convention enthusiastically endorsed Johnson as the party's nominee.

Yet there was still much more to come. Stevenson filed a federal case asking the court to put his own name on the general election ballot in place of

Johnson's! It was a wild move with virtually no law to back it up, but Stevenson's strategy wasn't really based on the law. The media attention on Box 13 had been intense, and papers like the *Dallas Morning News* that were very pro-Sevenson had been running headlines saying the election had been stolen. Stevenson's lawyers hoped those stories would be enough to induce the right judge to throw out Box 13 and, with it, Lyndon Johnson's nomination. It was a long shot, but it wouldn't be the first or the last time that a judge issued a ruling that had little to do with the law.

Stevenson's lawyers went over the list of federal judges in Texas and decided to file their case with Whitfield Davidson,[18] a reactionary whom they thought would be most likely to rule against the more liberal Johnson. They drove through the night and found Davidson as the sun came up on September 15 vacationing at a ranch in East Texas. He turned Texas politics inside out by signing an *ex parte* order restraining the Democratic Party from putting Johnson on the ballot and set the case for a hearing on September 21. Since there was no law to support Stevenson's case or Davidson's order, Johnson's lawyers confidently told him they would get the case dismissed at the hearing.

But what happened at the hearing left Johnson's lawyers shaken and their client apoplectic. Davidson not only denied their motion to dismiss the case, he entered an injunction forbidding "the preparation and distribution of ballots carrying Johnson's name for use in the election."[19] Johnson's legal team was so flummoxed they recommended that Johnson accept Davidson's suggestion that the two candidates "settle" the case by agreeing that *both* men's names go on the ballot in November. If Johnson didn't agree to that, they were afraid Davidson would keep Johnson off the ballot entirely. They still thought Stevenson's case had no legal merit, but they couldn't see a way to get Davidson's injunction reversed in time to save Johnson since the November ballots were about to be printed. A stay motion to the full Fifth Circuit would surely take too long.

It wasn't unusual for Johnson to get angry, but when his lawyers gave him their recommendation, he excoriated them as never before. He was not about to give away the victory he had won at the polls. Johnson had a team of fifteen to twenty lawyers in both Texas and Washington, as did Stevenson, but now he sought the counsel of one additional lawyer, Abe Fortas. Fortas was in private practice in Washington but had been in government positions before and had met Johnson, Connally, and several of the lawyers who were at the center of the campaign. Fortas had taught at the Yale Law School right after he graduated, and he was universally thought of as a whip smart lawyer. He was relatively young at thirty-eight but had experience in federal appeals, including cases in the Supreme Court.[20]

Fortas happened to be in Dallas taking depositions in a case and came to Fort Worth immediately to meet with Johnson. He saw a path to get Davidson's injunction vacated fast enough to keep Johnson on the ballot, a path no one else had suggested. Fortas' idea was to ask Supreme Court Justice Hugo Black to stay the injunction since a single justice can act with the full authority of the court on emergency applications for stays. Black had responsibility for all emergency matters that came up in the Fifth Circuit, which included Texas, and Fortas knew Black would rule on the application immediately. Fortas was also confident Black would rule for Johnson because the law was so clear. As he said years later, "There really was no question about the merits of the case. . . . [Judge Davidson] was just plain wrong."[21]

There was one procedural hurdle, though, before Johnson could go to Black. He would first have to ask the Fifth Circuit for a stay and *lose* there. To do that, Fortas recommended that Johnson file an application to stay with the single Fifth Circuit judge who would be most likely to rule *against* him. If they went to the full Fifth Circuit for a stay, rather than a single judge, too much time would be lost.

Fortas didn't have any doubts about what to do, but it was "difficult since Mr. Johnson had brought in all of these eminent lawyers who had different ideas, [and] I was an outsider and a youngster."[22] The more traditional, "by the book" lawyers were nervous, but Johnson didn't hesitate. He told them to do exactly what Fortas recommended.

They decided to present their stay application to Judge Joseph Hutcheson because he seemed most likely to deny the application quickly. Hutcheson had previously ruled that a single circuit judge acting alone should never stay a lower court injunction. The judge heard arguments from the lawyers in his chambers in Houston on Friday, September 24. When Hutchson ended the hearing with no indication of when he might rule, Johnson's lawyers wondered again about Fortas' strategy. But later the same day, their anxieties evaporated when Hutcheson ruled as Fortas predicted and denied Johnson's request. The road to Justice Black was open.

On Tuesday morning, September 28, Fortas and several other lawyers walked into Justice Black's elegant chambers in the Supreme Court building. Even for lawyers who have argued in the Supreme Court before, being there to present a case is always very special. It is impossible to escape the sense that you are playing a role in shaping the country's history. For Johnson's lawyers that morning, those feelings must have been especially acute since the success or failure of their motion would determine who would be a United States senator. The next day Justice Black stayed Davidson's injunction, and a week later the entire Supreme Court affirmed Black's ruling.[23]

Johnson was back on the ballot, and Stevenson was out of options. His lawyers complained bitterly about requesting a stay from Justice Black, but all Fortas did was follow normal Supreme Court procedure. Whatever happened in Jim Wells and other counties, Judge Davidson's injunction was lawless. Whether he acted out of a belief that he was doing the "right thing" regardless of the law, or whether he acted for some other reason is unknown. But the illegality of his ruling was clear. That was confirmed by the Fifth Circuit when it ultimately heard the case on appeal and ordered Stevenson's complaint dismissed because there was no legal basis for his claims.[24]

The impact of the 1948 Texas Senate election would prove to be enormous. Because Johnson went on from his Senate victory to become president, both American and world history followed a different course than they would have had Stevenson won. It is astonishing how several times during the few weeks from August 28 to September 29, the outcome of that Senate election oscillated between the candidates because of the decision of one man, a single vote on a committee, or one judge. Had just one of the Johnson votes on the State Democratic Executive Committee gone for Stevenson, the outcome would have been different. Had the Stevenson campaign simply noticed that Kinney and Hansford counties were not bothering to open the polls for the runoff, Stevenson would have won. Or if the judge in Austin had denied Johnson a temporary restraining order against the Jim Wells County Committee, Stevenson would have won. Had any of those things occurred, few people would know the name Lyndon Johnson today.

4

Jimmy Carter's 1962 Senate Race Almost Stole his Presidency

Jimmy Carter and Lyndon Johnson are two presidents with much in common. They were both Democrats, of course, and both men cared about equality and economic opportunity for those who had little. They came of age in essentially the same era, Johnson born in 1908 and Carter in 1924. They both grew up in rural parts of the South, though the land in Carter's southwest Georgia was relatively verdant and agriculturally productive, unlike the harsh Texas Hill Country, and Carter's father was a successful farmer and businessman, unlike Johnson's father.

The two fathers were opposites in other respects. Sam Johnson devoted much of his time to helping others and was elected to the state legislature six times with the hope of doing exactly that. He spent long hours driving around the sparse Texas countryside to tell farmers about the pensions they could apply for but were unaware of. By comparison, James Earl Carter Sr., Jimmy's father, showed little concern for the plight of poor people and remained unreconstructed on issues of race until his death. Jimmy Carter had some exposure to politics though his father, but nothing like the intense introduction that was Lyndon Johnson's. The elder Carter was elected to the state legislature in 1952 but served only a few months before dying of cancer.

The two presidents' paths to the White House differed as well, but they shared one thing in common—stolen senate elections. In Carter's case, it was a stolen state senate election in 1962. That Carter's senate election was stolen was not all that surprising given the dodgy nature of Georgia's elections at the time.

The Democratic Party was still the only significant political party in Georgia in 1962. An integral part of Georgia's one-party politics was that nearly everything was left to the party itself; almost no laws regulated primary elections. The Georgia Democratic Party set the procedures of the state primary election, and county Democratic committees had near-absolute power over local county elections. Abuse and election manipulations of every sort were rampant.

The situation was so chaotic and corrupt that Carl Sanders, who won the Democratic primary for governor in 1962, made election reform a key part of his campaign. Thirty years later, I tried a voting case that focused on the politics of that era, and I called Governor Sanders to testify. Sanders was only thirty-seven years old when he was elected governor, and his memory was still perfect. Many people think Sanders was the best governor Georgia ever had. He served at the same time that George Wallace was governor of Alabama, but they were opposites. Wallace was riding his "populist" racism to national prominence; Sanders was a progressive who would have none of that. When Wallace asked Sanders to address the Georgia General Assembly, Sanders refused. As he told me and later testified at trial, "I wasn't going to allow any of that kind of politics in Georgia if I could stop it."

When I called Sanders as a witness, the courtroom fell silent, and all eyes fixed on him as he strode to the witness stand. His testimony about Georgia's politics of 1962 painted a vivid picture of a time that many had forgotten and that younger people had never heard of.

> When I ran for Governor in 1962, one of my main campaign promises was election law reform. What we had was constantly abused by people who set

> the rules to benefit themselves. Except in a handful of counties where the General Assembly had passed local legislation that controlled, the rules for primary elections—which are the only ones that mattered then—were determined entirely by the local county democratic executive committees, which we called the "courthouse crowds" or the "courthouse gangs."
>
> They set the dates, times, and places for the elections, how, when and where to qualify to run, and whether the election would be by majority or plurality. Sometimes those fellows would set the time for qualifying way before the election so that, when an election came, someone who wanted to run would find out that it was too late. It was awful.

Another witness I called was George T. Smith, who had been speaker of the Georgia House of Representatives from 1962 until 1964 and then was elected lieutenant governor. He was a sitting justice on the Georgia Supreme Court when he testified in my case. Smith's life story was a page from the South's rural history. When he was young, he walked behind a mule plowing on the family farm, a farm later lost to the bank. Smith's family was so poor his mother used empty feed bags to make clothes for his sisters. He testified how it had been impossible in his own county to vote out a crooked sheriff because of the courthouse crowd's shenanigans. They paid a few people around the county to run for sheriff, and those pseudo candidates drew enough votes from family and friends to stop any serious challenger from winning a majority. The incumbent wouldn't get a majority either, but he came in first and won because the courthouse crowd said that a plurality was sufficient to win.

Aside from the "usual" skullduggery, the 1962 Georgia Senate races promised to be uniquely chaotic. For nearly 100 years, fifty-two of the state's fifty-four Senate districts consisted of three counties regardless of their population. Only Atlanta's Fulton County with its own senator and Savannah's Chatham County, paired with one other county, had more representation. The malapportionment was so extreme that one person's vote in the least populated Senate district had more than forty times the weight of a Fulton County voter.

Everything changed on March 26, 1962, when the Supreme Court ruled that malapportioned districts were unconstitutional. That decision ripped through Georgia and other states as decades of skewed politics were about to end. The local federal court in Atlanta that was hearing Georgia's redistricting case ruled that at least one chamber of the General Assembly, the House or the Senate, had to be redistricted for the upcoming election of legislators who would take office in January 1963. The court left it to the state to decide which chamber would be redistricted.

Many people from that era thought redistricting caused a greater revolution than desegregation, and when it came to political power they were surely right. Griffin Bell, who later served as U.S. Attorney General, was a judge on Georgia's redistricting court, and he commented that the Supreme Court's decision was not so much a "shock to the political establishment," it was "more like a funeral."[1]

The Democratic primary to nominate candidates for the General Assembly and statewide offices was held on September 12, 1962. But candidates for the General Assembly had no idea if winning would mean anything, since it was understood that a new election to nominate candidates, for either the Senate or the House, would be held under a radically different plan before the November general election.

As soon as the September primary was over, the incumbent governor, Ernest Vandiver, called the General Assembly into special session to work on a redistricting plan to satisfy the court's order. Hysterical cries rose from the counties that were about to lose their political advantage. Malapportionment was seen by rural people as their entitlement, and they were furious that they were about to be put on an equal footing with other voters. Brutal attacks were directed at the Supreme Court and Chief Justice Earl Warren, who were accused once again of "destroying our southern way of life," the refrain that rose from Southern whites when the Supreme Court had ruled school segregation unconstitutional in 1954.

When the General Assembly went into session, the House was adamant that it would not redistrict, but the Senate was a different story. Carl Sanders was the incumbent Senate president *pro tem* and wielded tremendous influence in that chamber even before his dominant victory in the race for governor on September 12. On the very first day of the session, it was clear that Sanders would convince the Senate to pass a redistricting plan,[2] and he accomplished exactly that in just a week's time. The bill was signed into law by Governor Vandiver on Friday afternoon, October 5. Candidates had to qualify immediately, by Tuesday, October 9, and the new primary would be held a week later on October 16. Georgia had accomplished in record time what some people said was impossible.

Everyone understood that the new law would rewrite the state's politics. Marion Gaines, a prominent journalist at the *Atlanta Constitution* who would later become the paper's first female editor, wrote: "Final enactment of the reapportionment bill marked the end of the most revolutionary series of changes to hit Georgia politics in any two-year period in history."[3]

While Gaines was certainly right about the revolutionary changes being wrought in Georgia, nowhere did old and new collide more dramatically than in the newly created 14th Senate district. It consisted of seven counties in the southwest corner of the state and included the tiny hamlet of Plains, Georgia, the home of Jimmy Carter. Like his father, Carter was a successful farmer and operated an agricultural business that served other farmers in the area and ginned cotton. He had never run for office before but had been appointed to the Sumter County Board of Education.

When the 14th district was created, it captured Carter's interest, and he thought he could run a strong race because of his personal and business connections in most of the district's seven counties. In addition, Sumter County, his home county, was the largest county in the district. Sumter had

24,650 residents, which was 35 percent of the entire district population. It was a very rural county, except for the county seat, Americus, a city of 13,500, but the other counties in the district made Sumter look like a busy urban center. Not only were they minimally populated, they were losing people at a remarkable pace, like most rural Southern counties. Four of the seven counties in the district had suffered 20 percent population declines since the previous census.

With the extremely compressed election schedule, Carter had no time to ponder whether to run or not. He qualified immediately and was opposed by one other man, Homer Moore. Moore's business background was a lot like Carter's, but unlike Carter he had run in the September primary and won. The senate district he won no longer existed, but Stewart County where he lived was in the new 14th district.

The least populous county in district 14 was Quitman County, a desperately poor, small patch of land only 170 square miles in size with 2,432 residents. It was added to district 14 in deference to a last-minute request by the man who represented Quitman in the House, Joe Hurst.[4] Quitman was so tiny, its inclusion had little impact on one-person, one-vote calculations, and Carter didn't think much about the county since it had so few voters. What Carter didn't know was that little Quitman County impacted elections far out of proportion to its size.

Joe Hurst was the archetype of the courthouse gang member that Sanders and Smith had testified about. He ran local politics and looked as if he had been cast for the part. He was sixty-two years old, a bit overweight, and usually wore a coat and tie with a fedora from a different time. Half a cigar jutted from his lips. He was the chairman of the Quitman County Democratic Executive Committee, and while he used that office to control elections, that was just the tip of his corruption and power.

Hurst's wife, Mary, was head of the county welfare office and had absolute power to decide whether people would get benefits or not. There were no legal services lawyers then to represent someone who had been denied the assistance they were entitled to. In impoverished Quitman County, that made a large percentage of the people dependent on the Hursts' good graces. To let people know just how dependent they were on the Hursts, their checks were not mailed to their residences but were sent to the Hursts, and Joe Hurst then delivered them personally to the payees. If there was anyone who missed the "suggestion" that they needed to do whatever Joe Hurst asked them to do if they wanted to get their check, he was never shy about making that explicit.

Long before the October 16 Senate race, Hurst was notorious for stuffing ballot boxes in Quitman County. He was so accustomed to election fraud in his little county that he was remarkably open about it. While the story didn't come out until years later, Hurst told the campaign manager for Homer Moore that he was going to stuff Quitman's ballot box for Moore. When told there was no need to do that since Moore was going to win anyhow, Hurst replied, "Well, we do it every time, and I don't want my people to get out of practice."[5]

Hurst was widely known as the man who could get a lot of votes for anyone whose district included Quitman County, and he had cultivated widespread influence by doing favors for others. In a testament to his influence, the General Assembly passed a law that allowed him to hold a paid position with the state even while he served in the General Assembly. The law violated Georgia's separation of powers prohibition, but it was ignored as a favor to Hurst.

Carter had none of Lyndon Johnson's well-honed political acumen when he ran for the Senate. He didn't see Hurst coming before election day, but he got a fast education in crooked courthouse politics on that one day. Soon after the polls opened, Carter got word of rampant irregularities in Quitman County. At the time, ordinaries were county officials who were responsible for probate and other matters, and in all but urban counties that had separate election boards, ordinaries were also responsible for general elections. Carter was told that voting was taking place in the tiny office of the Quitman County ordinary, Robert Ellis, where privacy was impossible. Not only was there no voting booth where ballots could be marked in secret, one of Hurst's confederates stood there to make sure people cast their votes for Moore. He brushed Carter off when challenged, saying, "I voted for Homer Moore and promised to politic for him, and I have a right to talk to people as I please."[6] Like Hurst, he had no fear that anyone could stop him.

Carter and his friends saw the same thing and worse at other Quitman precincts. More ballots were being put into the boxes than there were voters; pre-bundled ballots were put into ballot boxes; and ballots were sometimes removed from the boxes. Hurst's corruption infected those around him like a virus, and the disease spread beyond Quitman County. When Carter left a message for a reporter from nearby Columbus, he was crestfallen when he saw the reporter sharing a beer with Hurst in the middle of the election. The reporter later told Carter, "Everybody knows it's not right, but this is the way they always run elections over here."[7]

As the day went on, Carter's supporters saw a continuous stream of apparent fraud. To cover up the ballot box stuffing, campaign workers were adding to the list of voters random names of people who hadn't shown up to vote. It later turned out that sometimes Quitman voters were dead, while others were in prison.

Though he was shocked at what was happening in Quitman County, Carter worked intensely everywhere else in the district in the hope that the final total would give him the win regardless of Joe Hurst. As the votes were being tallied on election night, Carter had reason to celebrate. He won by a big margin in his home county, and with only Quitman County outstanding, he was ahead by seventy-five votes. Then his worst fears were realized. Moore beat Carter in Quitman by 360 votes to 136, a suspiciously high number given the number of actual voters in the county. Moore was declared the winner.

Carter met that evening with a few friends and the lawyer for Sumter County, but they were discouraging and for good reason. Georgia law was of no help; there was hardly any time before the general election and then it would be too late to challenge the primary; and with crooked politics going on for so long in Quitman County, why should they think that anyone would stop it now?

Carter may have been naive about local politics twenty-four hours earlier, but he was much less so that evening. He was also a man of determination, much like Lyndon Johnson. Regardless of what others said, Carter wasn't about to give up. He hired an Atlanta lawyer, Charles Kirbo, to find a way to right the wrong Joe Hurst had inflicted on him.

One path to challenge the election was to ask the Quitman County Democratic Executive Committee to set aside Quitman's count because of the irregularities. Although this would be a complete waste of time since Joe Hurst was the chairman of the committee, it was a step Carter had to take regardless. If he didn't, he could lose for not following all of the procedural rules. A hearing on Carter's petition was scheduled by the committee for Monday, October 29, but as soon as the committee convened, Moore's lawyer moved that Carter's petition be dismissed on "legal grounds." The committee promptly did exactly that without hearing a word of evidence. Carter was utterly livid. His supporters and his lawyers were equally appalled, and some wanted to give up the fight. But that was not who Jimmy Carter was.

Under the rules of the Georgia Democratic Party, Carter was allowed to appeal to the Georgia Democratic Party Executive Committee. An appeal had to be based on the evidentiary record, though, which was a problem since the county committee had not permitted any evidence! With nothing to lose, Carter appealed the county's "decision" to the State Party in the hope that someone in authority would condemn what had happened.

Carter could also ask for a recount, but that was problematic because recounts were designed for mistakes in counting ballots, not proving election fraud. Still, Carter again had nothing to lose so he asked for a recount which would take place before a panel of three people, one appointed by each candidate and the third the seniormost superior court judge from the adjoining judicial circuits. Given the presumed predilection of the candidates' designated panel members, the senior judge was the person who needed to be persuaded. In this case that was Judge Carl Crow, who had sat on other recount panels but never reversed the announced result of an election. Carter's recount petition asked the panel to throw out the box from Georgetown, the county seat of Quitman County. Their reason? The Georgetown box had 431 ballots, but only 333 persons had voted there.

By the time the panel was ready to hold the recount hearing, it was already November 1, just *five days* before the general election. If Carter didn't win immediately, he was done for. Georgia law didn't allow a primary election to be challenged after the general election occurred. To prepare for the hearing, Carter's team had obtained dozens of affidavits backing up his claims, and many of the people who gave affidavits came to the hearing to testify. As the hearing plodded on, Judge Crow said little and gave no indication of how he might rule. He was far more memorable for spitting streams of yellow-brown tobacco juice into the courtroom spittoon. Crow was a master of that art.

When the panel adjourned, Crow said they would have a decision the very next day, which was Friday, November 2, and he would render the decision at his courtroom forty miles away in Albany. The next morning, Carter was ecstatic when Crow announced that the panel had voted two to one to exclude all votes from the county's Georgetown box. With that box out, Carter would win the election with 2,811 votes to Moore's 2,746 votes.

Unfortunately for Carter, however, his seemingly conclusive win was about to become anything but conclusive. Moore immediately challenged the recount panel's decision before the Quitman County Democratic Executive Committee. While Moore was sure to win there, the county committee had no actual authority to rule on his appeal. The state party had the final authority to decide who was the rightful nominee under the circumstances. With just four days left before the general election, tactical arrows were flying in every direction. There was Moore's appeal to the county committee; two appeals to the state party, one by each candidate; a case by Carter before Superior Court Judge Tom Marshall to enjoin the Quitman County Committee from acting; and a petition to the secretary of state to have the ballots changed since they had been printed showing Moore as the Democratic nominee.

With Carl Sanders' resounding win in the September 12 gubernatorial primary, he had become the unquestioned locus of political power in Georgia. As he put it when I first spoke with him and he later testified, "I won the popular vote, I won the county unit vote, I won the white vote, and I won the black vote." He had appointed his close friend from Augusta, J. B. Fuqua, as chairman of the Democratic Party. Fuqua had grown up a poor sharecropper's son but had become a successful businessman and was on his way to becoming a billionaire at a time when billionaires weren't a dime a dozen like they are today. He had also just won the Democratic nomination for a state Senate seat in the October 16 primary.

The lawyers for both Carter and Moore knew they had to get to Fuqua or Sanders, or both, as soon as possible. Kirbo got there first. I knew Fuqua, as he was another of my witnesses in the same election case in which Sanders and Smith testified, and he told me about Kirbo and Carter. As Fuqua related those events to me, he received a frantic call from Kirbo asking to meet as soon as possible about the district 14 morass. Fuqua told Kirbo to come to his house in Augusta the next day, Saturday, November 3. At that meeting, Kirbo spread out on the floor of Fuqua's living room the proof that the Georgetown box had been stuffed to swing the vote to Moore. Fuqua was convinced but called Sanders before he made a final decision. Sanders told Fuqua, "Do what you think is right. If you think the election was stolen from Carter, name him our nominee." Fuqua did exactly that.

That was a gutsy move by Sanders. He knew about Hurst's political power and would not want to alienate a sitting member of the state House of Representatives if he could avoid it. Moreover, Carter was a political nobody at the time. Regardless, Sanders and Fuqua did the right thing.

Armed with the Democratic Party's certification naming Carter as the party's nominee, Kirbo faced yet another Herculean challenge with no time to spare. He had to convince the secretary of state, Ben Fortson, to order the seven county ordinaries to change their ballots for the Tuesday election. Fortson agreed and wired that instruction to the ordinaries. It was way too late to print new ballots, so county workers, members of Carter's family, and volunteers crossed out Moore's name and wrote in Carter's by hand on the printed ballots.

Once again, Carter and his supporters relaxed, finally sure of their victory. But once again, the sweet taste of victory immediately went sour. Carter's own pending case against the County Democratic Committee now threatened to drive a dagger into his candidacy. Moore's lawyers asked Judge Marshall to overrule Fortson's directive to the ordinaries and strike *all* names from the ballot, making the election a write-in contest. Legally, Marshall shouldn't do that because the Democratic Party had the authority to designate its nominees, but after all the trickery Carter had just endured, he was understandably anxious about Moore's latest ploy.

Hurst added to Carter's anxiety with a last-minute gambit even more outlandish than what the county committee had done before. On Saturday, the committee announced that it would have a hearing on Monday to hear the evidence "again," ignoring the fact that it had refused to hear any evidence at the original hearing. The committee also declared that the recount panel's decision in Carter's favor was suspended and would remain suspended until the committee made its decision—which would be sometime after the general election! The committee's action was completely without a legal foundation, but with time running out, confusion worked to Moore's advantage.

On Sunday afternoon, Carter's lawyers were told that Judge Marshall wanted to see everybody in his courtroom on Monday morning. That was an ominous sign for Carter. He was in as good a position as possible as the recognized nominee of the Democratic Party. Anything Marshall might do could only make matters worse for Carter.

When the candidates and their lawyers met with the judge on Monday, Marshall ordered the Quitman County Committee to stop interfering with the decision of the recount panel, which was good, but he gave no decision on the critical issue—who would be on the ballot, Carter or Moore? Instead, Marshall ordered the seven ordinaries to appear before him at 6:00 p.m. that same evening, a directive that bore only ill wind for Carter. When some of the ordinaries said they couldn't come because they had to prepare for the next day's election, Marshall had them arrested and brought to court.

Carter and his lawyers read the tea leaves and saw a catastrophe coming. Marshall wouldn't insist that the ordinaries come to court unless he was going to order them to do something, and it was hard to imagine that "something" working in Carter's favor. Carter's lawyer told him of the old saying about the power of a Georgia superior court judge: "They can close the banks in Atlanta, they can stop the ships in Savannah, and they can do anything else they damn well please." Carter was not amused.

The evening hearing went on and on until Marshall finally brought the arguments to a close after midnight. In less than seven hours the polls were set to open. Marshall announced his ruling and did exactly what Moore had asked. He ordered the ordinaries to strike the names of *both* candidates from the ballot. The election would now be a write-in contest that eliminated Carter's rightful position as the Democratic nominee. Carter was frustrated and more than a little disgusted with the judge's ruling, but there was nothing he could do at that point but live with it and hope for the best.

Robert Ellis, the Quitman County ordinary, was troubled by Hurst's election fraud and told Judge Marshall that a wrong had been committed that he wanted to fix if he could. Ellis went on to explain that he might have to disobey the judge's order and leave Carter's handwritten name on the ballots. "I have great respect for you as a judge," Ellis said, "but I want you to pray for me, because between here and Georgetown I'm going to decide what to do with this order you've given me."[8] Another ordinary who was similarly reluctant to follow Marshall's order told the judge, "I heard what you might do before I left home. I knelt down and asked the Lord for guidance, and I haven't heard from Him."[9] Marshall made clear that violating his order meant jail regardless of what the ordinaries might hear from the Lord.

Marshall later explained to a friend that he issued the order he did because there had been no proof of fraud outside of Quitman County, so everyone should just vote again. That was nonsense. Since no one had challenged the returns from any other county, they should have stood. The law was clear, too, that the Democratic Party had the right to determine its own nominees. Marshall probably ruled as he did more because of his personal relationship with Moore or some friends of Moore's.

The next day, election day, had been expected to be a non-event just twenty-four hours earlier, with Carter the Democratic nominee and no Republican on the ballot. But now, after Marshall's ruling, everyone in Carter's camp was beyond anxious, including Carter himself. Winning the election now meant winning a write-in campaign, something Carter hadn't anticipated. Turning out his supporters was essential, but that was harder than ever. People in south Georgia often didn't even bother to vote in general elections in 1962 since the elections were always decided in the Democratic primary. On top of that, with the lateness of Marshall's order, there was no time for Carter's team to explain to people about write-in voting. Confusion might determine who would win the election.

When the polls closed, though, the count was very much in Carter's favor: 3,013 to 2,180. Even the Quitman County vote was a pleasant surprise. Ellis had risked arrest and left Carter's name on the ballot. Hurst's courthouse gang was sobered by the weeks of controversy and the rumors of a federal vote fraud investigation, and nothing like the cheating of October 16 happened this time. With Hurst out of the picture and Carter on the ballet, the Quitman vote flipped to 448 votes for Carter and only twenty-three for Moore, a sure sign that people were tired of being pushed around by Hurst. In fact, Hurst did run into trouble for the election fraud he had committed in the first primary on September 16, 1962. Congressional candidates were on that ballot, which made the vote fraud a federal crime. Hurst was indicted and convicted, though only fined and given probation.[10]

But even with the convincing results on election day, Carter's fight to become a senator was still not close to over. Two of the ordinaries, those from Sumter and Quitman counties, had refused to take Carter's name off the ballot. No doubt, that had contributed to Carter's big lead in the election, and Moore announced that he was going to challenge the election because of this fact. Marshall was extremely angry that his order hadn't been obeyed and set the case for a hearing on November 30. Carter's lawyers told him that Marshall was so mad he was likely to order a new election with no names on the ballot; in other words, a write-in contest. Carter spent another three anxious weeks fearing what Marshall would do. He was amazed how a simple election had morphed into such a complicated, twisted saga. It seemed at times there had been more legal machinations in his three-week election fight than had occurred in all the decades of Dickens' *Bleak House*.

When the morning of the scheduled hearing came, to Carter's complete surprise Moore announced that he was dropping his case. It's impossible to know for certain why Moore did this, but Moore's lawyers likely told him that his case was ultimately not very strong. Even if Marshall ruled for him, which was likely, the Georgia Supreme Court would probably have reversed Marshall because his original order striking Carter's name from the ballot was plainly wrong.

Moore put his remaining hopes on a Hail Mary plea to the Georgia Senate, which under the Georgia Constitution had the ultimate authority to sit in judgment of its members' elections whenever a seat was contested. Carter worried about the influence Moore and his lawyers had in the Senate and wrote Sanders and others to plead his case, but this time his anxiety was unnecessary. When it came to Carter's turn to be sworn in and seated, no one questioned his election.

Carter should have realized that the Senate was very loyal to Sanders and Fuqua, now a senator himself. For the Senate to take up Moore's challenge to Carter's election would have run counter to what Sanders and Fuqua had done for Carter that Saturday in Augusta when they certified him as the party's nominee. No one was prepared to do that.

While Quitman County is a tiny, backwater Georgia county, a corrupt election there came extremely close to derailing the political career of a man who would ultimately become president of the United States. Had Carter failed in his 1962 Senate bid, the chance that he would have been elected Georgia's governor in 1970 would have been much less; maybe no chance at all. And without being Georgia's governor, he would never have become president.

One can wonder how many careers of other would-be politicians were snuffed out before they could bloom because of a crooked election. The answer is unknowable, but it is definitely not zero.

5

Two Centuries of Voter Suppression

Stuffing ballot boxes is a risky way to steal an election. There's no guaranty you'll succeed and there's always a chance you might get caught. A much more reliable way to steal elections is to fix the rules so that some people just aren't allowed to vote. Elections have been stolen that way throughout the country's history.

Voting is much more inclusive today than in 1788, but the struggle over the right to vote is still very much with us, bitter as always. People who want more accessible voting are in a struggle with those who want to restrict voting, and both sides are fervent in their cause.

Having fought a war with Britain to gain independence and the right to elect their own representatives, one might have expected the men who wrote the Constitution to enshrine the right to vote in that founding document. But it was not to be. Inspired by Rousseau and the French Enlightenment, Thomas Paine was a fierce advocate for suffrage: "The right of voting for representatives is the primary right by which other rights are protected. To take away this right is to reduce a man to slavery." Others at the convention were advocates for liberal suffrage, but they were hardly the only voice. James Madison warned against giving the vote to people who were not freeholders—that is, owners of real property.

> The freeholders of the Country would be the safest depositories of Republican liberty. In future times a great majority of the people will not only be without land, but any other sort of property. These will either combine under the influence of their common situation; in which case, the rights of property & the public liberty, will not be secure in their hands or, which is more probable, they will become the tools of opulence & ambition, in which case there will be equal danger on another side.[1]

Notwithstanding Madison's parsimonious view of who should vote, he believed the right to vote was so important it should be permanently fixed in the Constitution. "The right of suffrage is certainly one of the fundamental articles of republican Government and ought not to be left to be regulated by the Legislature." But as finally written and ratified, that is exactly what the Constitution did—left to the legislators *of the states* the responsibility to dictate who could vote.

The Constitution granted the right to vote for congressional representatives (and later senators when the 17th Amendment was ratified in 1913) and required that every state have a "Republican Form of Government," but the crucial question of *who* could vote was assigned to the states for both state *and* federal elections. The only limitation on the election of congressional representatives was that they be elected by the voters "in each State [who] have the Qualifications requisite for Electors of the most numerous Branch of the State Legislature."

Ironically, it was likely a good thing that the drafters of the Constitution were silent about who could vote. The idea of universal suffrage and a truly democratic vote would not have been endorsed by a majority of the delegates to the convention. If they had specified who could vote, the result would have become an embarrassment.

By deferring to the states, voting was initially restricted to a small number of wealthy white men. Only 6 percent of the population were eligible to vote in the first presidential election in 1788–9,[2] but opposition to the freeholder requirement soon grew too loud to ignore. Madison was right that the number of propertyless people would exceed those with property in the future, though he likely didn't foresee that the "future" would arrive so soon. It did when large numbers of poor immigrants fled Europe and Britain for the United States and joined forces with progressive freeholders to demand a change. In 1792 New Hampshire became the first state to drop its freeholder requirement.

Most other states, influenced by Jeffersonian and Jacksonian democracy, dropped their property ownership requirements in the early 1800s. Generally, the changes were peaceful, but Rhode Island was a glaring exception. There, the landed class refused to give up their advantage until the opposing sides clashed in the Dorr War.

The Republican Guaranty Clause required that every state adopt a constitution with a republican form of government when it joined the Union. They all did except Rhode Island, which refused to abandon its original 1663 Royal Charter, described by the Rhode Island Supreme Court as "the definition of despotism."[3]

The Royal Charter had plenty of flaws, but restricting voting to freeholders was especially obnoxious as the state became urbanized. The many immigrants who populated the cities rarely owned real property, and hostility by the freeholder elite to reform got ugly. They argued that broader suffrage would lead to dishonesty and fraud, which was profoundly hypocritical since the existing freeholder system fostered blatant fraud. One notorious example was the wealthy Sprague family who employed thousands of poor millworkers. The Spragues gave their employees deeds for just enough land to meet the freeholder requirement to vote, instructed their workers who to vote for, then took the deeds back as soon as the election was over.[4]

The conflict with the ruling freeholders came to a boil in 1841 when the Rhode Island Suffrage Association called a mass meeting to set up a new government, elect representatives, and draft a constitution that eliminated the freeholder requirement. The People's Constitution was approved in a referendum that freeholders denounced as illegal. The incumbent governor—whose name, "King," could not have been better scripted—and leading freeholders created the Law and Order Party, a branding ploy copied many times up to the present. Some members of the Suffrage Party gave up the cause when King threatened their arrest, but it was able to put together a full slate of candidates for elections and elected Thomas Dorr governor. The battle lines were drawn since King and the Charter government were unwilling to compromise, and outright war seemed unavoidable.

Dorr and an armed militia marched through the capital of Providence to hold their first legislative session. The Law and Order government responded by arresting people for the "crime" of being elected to the new legislature. The Dorr War had become a major national issue, and Dorr met with President John Tyler and others in Washington to discuss a solution, to no avail. Back in Providence, Dorr was greeted as a hero by thousands, many of them armed militiamen, but he was stymied politically. He decided to break into the state arsenal to seize rifles, ammunition, and heavy artillery, but unfortunately for Dorr, the plan was leaked to the opposition. On the night set for action, the Law and Order Party lay in wait for the "secret" assault. Realizing there was no hope of military success, Dorr ordered his forces disbanded to avoid pointless bloodshed.

In 1842, a new constitution was finally approved by the incumbent government that gave native-born adult males the right to vote regardless of property, and a war was avoided. While the rebellion in Rhode Island was unique, the demand for increased suffrage was spreading everywhere. In 1856, North Carolina was the last state to eliminate a blanket freeholder requirement,[5] though they were revived after the Civil War to keep African Americans from voting. Many local governments continued to require property ownership to vote and hold office until those requirements were struck down by the Supreme Court in 1969.[6]

The right to vote and the suffragettes

When the Constitution was ratified, the rights of women were stuck in the Middle Ages. English common law was incorporated into state laws, and it subjected married women to the law of "coverture." From the moment a woman was married, what rights she had were subsumed under her husband. She couldn't own property or enter into contracts, and her earnings belonged to her husband. Any personal property she had, whether a little or a vast inheritance, passed to her husband when she married. Real property did not technically pass to her husband unless he survived her, but from the moment they were married he had absolute control over any real property she owned at the time of the marriage. Had the Constitution prescribed who could vote, women would have been excluded given the archaic views of the day and the fact that all fifty-five delegates to the Constitutional Convention were men.

In the early years of the country, voting by women was rare but not unheard of. New Jersey was unique among the original states in not restricting the franchise to men. Its 1776 constitution granted the vote to "all inhabitants" who were "worth Fifty Pounds" and of "full age."[7] Since there was no gender restriction, women voted over the objection of some people that women weren't meant by "all inhabitants." To address that objection, several subsequent laws were passed that explicitly allowed New Jersey women to vote.

Even though there was little objection to women voting in New Jersey, female suffrage fell victim to the work of a vindictive legislator, John Condit. Women had supported Condit's opponent, and he was eager to take the vote away from them. He saw his opportunity to do that in the wake of a comically fraudulent referendum in 1806 concerning the location of a new Essex County courthouse. Men and boys voted in the referendum regardless of their qualifications and were carted around to vote repeatedly at multiple polls. People from outside the county were brought in to pad the vote, and women and girls joined the fraud and voted again and again like their male counterparts.

The Essex County election fraud happened to coincide with the beginning of New Jersey's legislative session, and the clamor to "do something" about vote fraud resonated throughout the state. Unfortunately for New Jersey's women, Condit was the primary advocate for an election "reform" bill that, among other things, stripped the vote from "females," "persons of color," "aliens," and "negroes."[8] Like the voices for voter suppression today, Condit justified his bill on the ground that it was intended to prevent "fraud," even though none of the targeted groups had been responsible for the Essex County fraud which had been instigated by the white men who controlled the local politics. Nevertheless, Condit's bill passed and women would not vote again in New Jersey for 113 years.

There was hope that the 14th Amendment might bring women legal equality since it prohibited states from denying *all* people "equal protection of the law," but those hopes were dashed by the Supreme Court in an opinion by Justice Bradley upholding an Illinois statute that prohibited women from practicing law:

> The constitution of the family organization, which is founded in the divine ordinance, as well as in the nature of things, indicates the domestic sphere as that which properly belongs to the domain and functions of womanhood . . . [T]he family institution is repugnant to the idea of a woman adopting a distinct and independent career from that of her husband . . . The paramount destiny and mission of woman are to fulfill the noble and benign offices of wife and mother. This is the law of the Creator.[9]

The long road to female suffrage had only occasional, partial victories at first. Kentucky allowed women to vote on county school issues under an 1838 law, but no state or territory granted women an equal right of suffrage until sixty-two years after New Jersey's reversal. Wyoming was the first in 1869 under its territorial legislature, but female suffrage in Wyoming was threatened when it petitioned Congress for statehood in 1890. The territory's delegation was told statehood was doubtful unless they ended female voting, but Wyoming's all-male territorial legislature responded bluntly: "We will stay out of the Union a hundred years rather than come in without our women."[10] Congressional opposition wilted just enough in the face of Wyoming's resolute stance, and in 1890 it became the first state that granted women full suffrage.

A few other states followed suit, but the suffrage movement realized that their right to vote would always be at risk without a constitutional amendment that enfranchised women for *all* elections on the same basis as men. What would become the 19th Amendment was introduced in the Senate in 1878 but wasn't even taken up for a vote until 1887 when it was defeated by thirty-four votes to sixteen. The first vote in the House wasn't until 1915, twenty-eight years later. It was defeated there, too, but the vote wasn't as lopsided—174 in favor and 204 opposed.

The politics of suffrage changed as a result of the skillful organization and advocacy of suffragettes under the leadership of the National American Woman Suffrage Association. The most ridiculous arguments that had been used against suffrage in the past disappeared, like the absurd claim that voting would cause female infertility because of the mental exertion.[11] The old argument that women were not equipped for politics became laughable in the face of the suffragettes' political skills. Still, many men and women continued to adhere to Justice Bradley's antediluvian view of women and their "proper place."

The challenge of amending the Constitution was enormous. It required approval by two-thirds of both the House and the Senate and three-quarters of the then forty-eight states. When the amendment was finally approved by Congress on June 4, 1919, only fifteen states gave women full voting rights. The anti-suffrage opposition had dedicated supporters and was well funded, in part by liquor interests that were afraid women voters would boost the temperance movement.

Congress' approval of the 19th Amendment came after decades of planning and political preparation, however. Never before or since has there been such an effective, well-executed national political campaign. An important part of the suffragettes' strategy was to push for quick ratification so women could vote in the 1920 presidential election. The possibility of millions of new voters motivated the leadership of both national political parties to support ratification in the hope they would be rewarded at the polls.

A ratification resolution was introduced in Illinois the day after Congress acted and it passed on June 10, followed immediately by five more states. Five days after Congress had acted, ten legislatures currently in session had committed to ratification and another four that were scheduled to be in session by January 1920 were certain to ratify. Massachusetts was the eighth state to ratify, and it was especially gratifying because it was the home of one of the biggest anti-suffrage associations in the country. It was also the birthplace of Lucy Stone and Susan B. Anthony, two of the most important suffragettes.

Texas was the first southern state to consider ratification, and the fight there was vicious. As the debate went on and the opposition began to lose ground, six opposition senators went so far as to offer to resign their seats if ten other opposition senators would join them, the loss of sixteen senators being enough to defeat a quorum and prevent the legislature from acting. In a dramatic vote, three senators who had been in the opposition switched sides, and Texas' ratification resolution passed on June 28. Success in conservative Texas added to the suffragettes' optimism that they would succeed.

By the summer of 1920, thirty-five states had ratified and eight had voted down ratification. Of the remaining five states, North Carolina and Florida were in the anti-suffrage camp, which left only three states where the final 36th ratification was possible: Connecticut, Vermont, and Tennessee. Connecticut and Vermont were both favorable, but neither one was in session, and their governors were adamantly opposed to calling a special session. Tennessee became the last hope for ratification before the 1920 election. When President Wilson intervened, Tennessee's governor finally relented and called a special session.

The Tennessee Senate quickly ratified, and the suffragettes' poll of the House was favorable, but with a caveat. They had a separate list of legislators who were reputed to be bribable, and when it came to a vote, all eight of the pro-suffrage legislators on the bribable list switched sides. The Tennessee House was knotted at forty-eight to forty-eight, and the suffragettes' hope depended on a single twenty-four-year-old legislator, Harry Byrne. Byrne had told the suffragettes he felt constrained to vote against the amendment because that is how his constituents felt, but if his vote became necessary for passage, he would vote to ratify. Byrne stuck to his word and made a brief but historic speech on the House floor:

> I want to state that I changed my vote in favor of ratification first because I believe in full suffrage as a right; second, I believe we had a moral and legal right to ratify; third, I know that a mother's advice is always safest for her boy to follow, and my mother wanted me to vote for ratification; fourth, I appreciated the fact that an opportunity such as seldom comes to a mortal man to free 17 million women from political slavery was mine.[12]

The amendment was ratified with Byrne's vote, and he became a hero to the suffragette movement.

The first organized meeting calling for female suffrage was the Seneca Falls Convention in 1848, seventy-two years before the 19th Amendment was finally ratified. At Seneca Falls, many women and men believed that the American ideals of democracy would lead the country to be the first to give the vote to women. But by 1920, twenty-six other countries had already done so while the United States remained stuck in Justice Bradley's past and two more generations of American women despaired.

Two centuries of Black voter suppression

Racial discrimination has always been part of the history of the United States. Slavery was incorporated in the Constitution, and African Americans were subjected to the brutal world of Jim Crow and denied the right to vote until the later part of the twentieth century. But what many people don't realize is that there was nothing inevitable about the racial horrors that happened after the Civil War. To the contrary, they were largely the result of Supreme Court decisions that took the life out of the 13th, 14th, and 15th Amendments that had been passed to end slavery and "protect the newly-made freeman and citizen from the oppressions of those who had formerly exercised unlimited dominion over him."[13]

Each of the amendments included a provision that expressly authorized Congress to pass "appropriate legislation" to achieve the amendment's goals, and the Reconstruction Congress used that authority to enact a series of laws to ensure that the four million newly freed slaves and half million African Americans who were already free enjoyed the *full* rights of citizenship. One of those laws, the Enforcement Act of 1870, criminalized violence and conspiracies to deprive people of their lawful rights. Prosecutions were so successful under that law that the Ku Klux Klan was effectively eliminated in South Carolina in 1871–2 after hundreds of Klansmen were convicted.[14]

Tragically, federal efforts to combat the KKK were ended when the Supreme Court ruled that the Enforcement Act was unconstitutional because Congress was supposedly powerless to criminalize violence unless the perpetrators were "state officers."[15] Violence by private persons to prevent African Americans from voting was deemed to be beyond Congress' power. To come to that conclusion, the court ignored its long-standing practice that it should defer to Congress' judgment about what legislation is "appropriate." It also ignored the fact that the Enforcement Act was passed by most of the same legislators who had drafted the Civil War amendments. Because of that, the court normally would say that the Enforcement Act was proof of what Congress meant by "appropriate legislation" when it wrote those amendments. It skipped that rule to get to the conclusion it wanted.

In a pair of contradictory decisions that had devastating consequences, the court ruled, first, that a Louisiana civil rights law that prohibited discrimination in "public conveyances" like ferries and trains was unconstitutional because only Congress could regulate public commerce. The court then turned around in the *Civil Rights Cases* and declared unconstitutional the federal Civil Rights Act of 1875 that prohibited discrimination in the very same kind of public, commercial businesses like ferries and trains that the court had just said were exclusively for Congress to regulate![16] Justice Harlan's dissenting opinion eloquently criticized the court's refusal to allow Congress the power and authority that was necessary to enforce the Constitution:

> The opinion in these cases proceeds . . . upon grounds entirely too narrow and artificial. The substance and spirit of the recent amendments of the Constitution have been sacrificed by a subtle and ingenious verbal criticism. "It is not the words of the law but the internal sense of it that makes the law. The letter of the law is the body; the sense and reason of the law is the soul." Constitutional provisions, adopted in the interest of liberty, and for the purpose of securing, through national legislation, if need be, rights inhering in a state of freedom, and belonging to American citizenship, have been so construed as to defeat the ends the people desired to accomplish, which they attempted to accomplish, and which they supposed they had accomplished by changes in their fundamental [constitutional] law.

In 1896, thirteen years after that decision, the court took the final step and upheld *state mandated segregation* in *Plessy vs. Ferguson*.[17] While Justice Harlan saw the tragic consequences of the Supreme Court's decisions in his time, one has to wonder if he ever imagined that it would be ninety years before the *Civil Rights Cases* would be superseded (but never reversed even to this day)[18] when the Supreme Court upheld the 1964 Civil Rights Act that prohibited racial discrimination in places of public accommodation.

That *Plessy* was based on the justices' personal, subjective views, rather than what the law said, is apparent from the court's own words describing the limit of state legislative power: "[The state's] police power must be reasonable and extend only to such laws as are enacted in good faith for the promotion of the public good, and not for the annoyance or oppression of a particular class." How, then, was it possible that mandating segregation was within the state's "police power"? Only because the majority of justices believed that preserving white supremacy was a "public good" in spite of the Civil War amendments that were predicated on the opposite premise.

The justices' private words also make clear that they were driven by personal racial bias, not by any neutral interpretation of the Constitution. The opinion in the *Civil Rights Cases* was written by Justice Bradley, whose candid thoughts on integration were expressed in a letter he wrote to Justice Woods in which he complained that prohibiting segregation was tantamount to enslaving white people. "To deprive white people of the right of choosing their own company would be to introduce another kind of slavery."[19]

After these decisions, the country sank into the world of Jim Crow that crushed the lives of millions of Americans and left lasting scars on the character of the nation that remain with us today. As historian C. Vann Woodward and others have shown, that world was not at all inevitable. It required the racism of the Supreme Court justices, who fanned and fostered the worst tendencies of the worst white people. Those decisions enabled racial discrimination and oppression when they struck down federal laws that would have prohibited Jim Crow from ever taking root. The court's decisions also had an effect beyond their repugnant legal rules. They added a crucial imprimatur of moral legitimacy. It is often said that the Supreme Court cannot legislate morality, which is true, but it assuredly can articulate moral principles that become part of the character of the nation.

The Supreme Court's decisions on voting rights were equally dreadful. After Reconstruction, Black men voted in much of the South for another generation, but they were systematically eradicated from politics at the end of the nineteenth and beginning of the twentieth centuries when the court neutered the protections of the Civil War amendments and congressional legislation.

One case from 1898, *Williams vs. Mississippi*,[20] is among the worst in the Supreme Court's Hall of Shame. The 1890 Mississippi Constitutional Convention was held for the specific purpose of creating a new constitution to keep Black men from voting. There was no secret to the convention's mission—it was openly promoted as the "Disfranchisement Convention"—and it subjected Mississippians to a raft of new requirements, like poll taxes and literacy tests, that would keep many more Black men from voting than whites. When the Mississippi constitution came before the U.S. Supreme Court, there was no question why it had been adopted. Mississippi's Supreme Court had answered that and explained in detail how it went about excluding Black voters. The Disfranchisement Convention, the court said, had "swept the circle of expedients to obstruct the exercise of the franchise by the negro race."[21]

The Mississippi Supreme Court listed some of those "expedients," which ran from gerrymandering the legislature to the voter qualifications that were challenged in the *Williams* case. Those qualifications were designed, the Mississippi court explained, to disqualify voters based on "certain peculiarities" that were more common among Blacks "by reason of [their] previous condition of servitude and dependence." Those "peculiarities" that resulted from slavery included indigency. Because "landless" Black laborers changed residence more often than landed whites, voters who moved out of their "election precinct, though only to an adjoining farm, were declared ineligible [to vote] . . . for a year." The poll tax was adopted to be "a clog upon the franchise" for Black men. Less serious crimes that Black men were charged with more often than whites disqualified a man from voting, but more serious crimes "in which violence was the principal ingredient were not" disqualifying because, according to the Mississippi court, those crimes were much more likely to be "white men's crimes."

If anyone wondered why the Mississippi Constitution focused on the "peculiarities" of Black men rather than simply prohibiting them from voting, the Mississippi Supreme Court explained that as well. It was done for fear that such an explicit attack could be tripped up by the 15th Amendment. "Restrained by the federal constitution from discriminating against the negro race, the convention discriminates against its characteristics," the Mississippi court wrote. It was hoped that that its less "explicit" attack on Black voters might slip by the U.S. Supreme Court.

The Mississippi court was right. The U.S. Supreme Court upheld Mississippi's disenfranchisement provisions because none of them *expressly* disqualified Black men. That both the *admitted purpose and effect of the laws* were to eliminate Black voters was of no concern. After reciting Mississippi's admissions of why and how its voting laws worked, the U.S. Supreme Court said:

> If weakness were to be taken advantage of, it was to be done within the field of permissible action under the limitations imposed by the federal constitution, and the means of it were the alleged characteristics of the negro race . . . . [T]he operation of the [Mississippi] constitution and laws is not limited by their language or effects to one race.

Regardless of the "sinister intention" behind the law, "black men as well as white men" had the same right "under the law" to avoid disqualification. That was enough to satisfy the justices' absurd view of the 15th Amendment.

The *Williams* opinion threw out a bone by saying it was not addressing the possibility that Mississippi's rules were administered discriminatorily. But any hope that discriminatory enforcement of voting laws might be stopped was promptly snuffed out a few years later in *Giles vs. Harris.*[22] The local registrar had refused to register Giles because he was Black, and Giles sought a federal order to add him to the voter list. In another shameful opinion, the Supreme Court said that this wasn't the kind of thing federal courts do. Nothing, the court ruled, would be gained by "making the court a party to the unlawful [voter registration] scheme by accepting it and adding another voter to its fraudulent lists."

With these decisions on the books, the 15th Amendment was a dead letter, and there was nothing to restrict racist elements in the South from crushing

Black political power. One voter suppression law after another was passed, and Black voter registration declined precipitously in the first decade of the twentieth century.[23] Literacy tests were a general requirement, and they had a devastating effect. While there were plenty of illiterate whites in the South, too, it had been criminal to teach slaves to read and write, and education for Black people was virtually nonexistent after the Civil War.

Discrimination in applying literacy tests, understanding tests, and good character qualifications for voting were rampant. The kinds of questions that were put to prospective voters to test whether they "understood the duties and obligations of citizenship" were subjective enough that registrars could reject anyone they wanted to. In a case I argued in the Supreme Court, I commented that "No member of the bar of this Court could have passed the test Georgia had." Justice Thurgood Marshall responded by asking, "Didn't they ask how many windows were in the White House?" I had never heard of that one, but I have no doubt he was correct.

Poll taxes weren't a new creation and had even been used as a significant revenue-raising device in some colonial governments. But they sprung up throughout the South after the Supreme Court let it be known they would be upheld no matter how heavily they impacted Black people. Property ownership requirements that had disappeared before the Civil War reappeared in the South. Voter registration books were closed months before elections, and even when they were open, registration was limited in many places to a couple of hours one day a week. Registration was done at the county courthouse, which became more and more a symbol of racist injustice, and that alone deterred Black people from registering. Fear was also a well-honed weapon to keep African American voters from registering. There were rural counties in every state in the South in which trying to register could be physically dangerous and financially costly. A loan might be called, furniture repossessed, or the sheriff mighty show up unannounced for an eviction if a Black person was getting "too political."

As Republicans, populists, and other political movements receded, the South became a one-party region where only the Democratic Party mattered. African Americans were formally excluded from politics with the adoption of the Democratic white primary. Incredibly, the Supreme Court *upheld* the white primary so long as it was "only" mandated by the party, not by the state itself.[24]

None of this would have happened if the Supreme Court had not so narrowly interpreted the Civil War amendments and improperly restricted Congress' authority to pass legislation under those amendments. The court had killed the roots of the 13th, 14th and 15th Amendments before they ever had a chance to fulfill their transformative mission.

It wasn't until 1944 that the Supreme Court reversed itself and invalidated white primaries.[25] That sparked Black political activity in Southern cities and in some rural areas as well. But it was another twenty years of voter registration campaigns, marches, and suffering the brutality of local law enforcement and a revived Ku Klux Klan before the Voting Rights Act of 1965 was passed.

Among other things, the Act banned all "tests or devices" as a prerequisite to voting in areas of the country with a history of rampant discrimination, which meant the entire South. Of equally great importance was the preclearance requirement of Section 5 that prohibited those same states from making any change in their election procedures without *first* obtaining federal approval, either from the Attorney General or by proving to the D.C. District Court that the proposed change was non-discriminatory.

Poll taxes had remained in force in four states, all members of the former Confederacy (Alabama, Mississippi, Texas, and Virginia), but they were banned in federal elections when the 24th Amendment was ratified in 1964. Then the Supreme Court struck them down for all elections because "wealth or fee paying has . . . no relation to voting qualifications."[26]

In a very few years, counties that had allowed no Black registered voters changed dramatically, and by the early 1970s, registration rates between Blacks and whites were not very different in most areas. That's when I came to the

South as a young lawyer. I was struck by the huge gap between Black voter registration and Black representation on city councils, county commissions, school boards, and in the legislatures. In Georgia, there were fewer than a dozen Black elected officials in the state out of more than 3,000. The reason was simple. Regardless of the percentage of Black people in the local population, all the candidates were elected from a large enough area that the majority of the voters were white. In a city that was 35 percent Black, for example, every seat on the city council was elected citywide. Black voters were outvoted by the white majority and unable to elect *any* candidate. This wasn't unique to Georgia; it was true across the South.

The discriminatory impact of these voting systems was so obvious, I didn't think even the increasingly conservative Supreme Court could ignore such prejudice. I knew the courts wouldn't invalidate an election system "just because" Blacks hadn't been elected; I would have to prove more. Myself and several other lawyers thought we could win if we proved that Black voters were denied a meaningful political voice in an at-large election because of racism in the community.

The first case I filed that went to trial was against Albany, Georgia, which was notorious as the only city that Martin Luther King, Jr. came to desegregate but left defeated. The federal judge who had presided over that area of the state for years was an unreconstructed segregationist (J. Robert Elliott, Herman Talmadge's old Floor Leader), and it would have been impossible to win with him. But Albany had been reassigned recently to a new judge, Wilbur D. Owens, Jr.

The case took a big turn in our favor when the evidence proved that Albany had switched from district elections to citywide elections right after the white primary was struck down in 1946. The change was made to cancel out the power of the newly enfranchised Black voters in a district where they were a majority and could elect a commissioner of their choosing. The judge ruled for my clients because of that history, but didn't buy the broader "vote dilution" theory. Still, it was an exhilarating win for me as a young lawyer, and a far more meaningful win for Albany's Black citizens who now had the power to elect commissioners they chose. A few months after the trial, there were two Black city commissioners in Albany for the first time in history.

Both sides appealed, the city contesting the judgment in its entirety and my clients trying to get a better election plan. Even the conservative judges then on the Fifth Circuit were not like the obtuse right-wingers there today, and I drew a good panel that adopted the vote dilution theory as a way to challenge the constitutionality of at-large elections regardless of how and why they had been adopted. With that precedent, I and other lawyers set about filing similar voting cases, sometimes winning, sometimes losing and appealing, and sometimes getting a decent settlement.

While Southern political systems were being desegregated slowly but surely with these cases, the Supreme Court shocked everyone in 1980 when it decided *City of Mobile vs. Bolden*,[27] which was as wrong-headed as the court's voting rights decisions a century earlier. Both the trial court and the Fifth Circuit had found overwhelming evidence that Black voters in Mobile were shut out of politics because of the citywide voting structure, but that wasn't enough for the Supreme Court. The court said that the plaintiffs were out of luck unless they could also prove that at-large voting was used for the specific *purpose* of discriminating.

The decision was infuriating because the court had ruled again and again, for nearly two centuries, that the motive behind a law had nothing to do with its constitutionality. In cases like *Williams vs. Mississippi*, where there was clear proof that the state's voting restrictions were racially motivated, the court said the state's motive was irrelevant. But now, in *Mobile*, the rule was the opposite—the failure to prove that racism was the very reason why citywide elections were used was fatal. The only thing consistent in the cases was that Black voters lost.

Stewart wrote the opinion and said the 15th Amendment was irrelevant so long as Black people could physically cast a ballot. The court had erased the word "abridge" from the amendment's prohibition against states "denying *or abridging*" the right to vote on account of race. The Mobile case was rule by fiat, nothing more. The justices who joined Stewart simply wanted to put an end to vote dilution cases; they weren't concerned how they did it or whether their "legal analysis" held water. Stewart disingenuously wrote, "If there's a problem, there may be a remedy," but it wasn't to integrate the election process with a constitutional case. That sounded like the *Giles* opinion from eighty years earlier.

Since the 1950s, there had been real progress because of the Supreme Court's leadership that was helping dismantle white supremacy, but that leadership had come to a close with the Republican Southern Strategy that traded electoral votes for a presidential commitment to appoint Supreme Court justices who would undo as much of the Warren court's rulings as possible. The *Bolden* decision was a direct result of that insidious deal. Southern whites who were furious about desegregation had won, and their Faustian bargain had paid off.

Bolden brought an immediate halt to new at-large election cases. Community leaders across the South who wanted to bring vote dilution cases in their cities were stunned. They had grown up seeing the Supreme Court as the one place where Black people could go that would say "No" to white supremacists. Now, suddenly, the court had switched sides.

The week after *Bolden* was decided, I met with Congressman Don Edwards, who chaired the House Subcommittee on Civil and Constitutional Rights. Also at the meeting were representatives from civil rights groups and four or five other lawyers who had tried voting cases. Edwards wanted to learn more about the effect of *Bolden* and discuss possible legislation to fix the problem *Bolden* created. Everyone agreed that further progress in breaking down political white supremacy was at an end so long as *Bolden* was the final word. Edwards committed to do everything he could to get legislation passed but could make no assurance it would be possible. The target date for legislation was 1982 because certain parts of the Voting Rights Act were up for renewal that year and voting rights would be on the legislative calendar.

Whatever the prospects for legislation had been when we met in May, they looked much worse after the 1980 November election. Reagan took the White House from Carter, and he was openly hostile to civil rights. It was in August of that same year that Reagan went to Philadelphia, Mississippi, to give his infamous "states' rights" speech. States' rights, of course, was the battle cry for ending federal civil rights protection of every kind. The town where Reagan spoke was a national symbol for the Ku Klux Klan. It was the location where the Klan had murdered voter registration volunteers a few years earlier. White Southerners got Reagan's message. So did Black people.

Just as bad were the changes in Congress—thirty-five seats switched from Democrat to Republican in the House, and even conservative Southern Democrats in the Senate were defeated by hard-core Republican right-wingers. Still, we pressed on.

At the same time, I had voting cases pending when *Bolden* was decided that I had already tried and were on appeal. One of them was against the Burke County Board of Commissioners, and the trial judge, Anthony Alaimo, had written an extremely strong opinion in our favor. I rejoiced when the Fifth Circuit affirmed Alaimo in spite of *Bolden* and didn't think the Supreme Court would agree to hear Burke County's appeal since it takes fewer than a hundred of the thousands of petitions for review it gets each year. But I was wrong. The court agreed to hear the county's appeal and set the case for argument in February of 1982.

Lawyers who followed civil rights litigation were nearly unanimous that we would lose because of *Bolden*, but I thought I saw a path to win. I assumed I would get the original three dissenters from the Mobile case—White, Marshall, and Brennan—and I also thought I would get Blackmun even though he was with the majority in *Bolden*. His problem was more with the remedy in that case than the underlying claim, and I didn't have a remedy problem in my case.

I also thought I might be able to get Burger because sometimes he accepted a trial court's findings of fact when the other conservatives ignored them to get to the result they wanted. Judge Alaimo's findings were powerful, maybe powerful enough to sway Burger. But the real wild card was Sandra Day O'Connor who had just replaced Stewart. She was a conservative Reagan appointee and largely unknown, but I felt she couldn't be worse than Stewart.

The argument went as well as it possibly could. Rehnquist asked a very tough question about Judge Alaimo's opinion, but I was ready for it and my answer made what could have been a fatal issue disappear. Rehnquist didn't say anything else after that. Powell was frustrated that I had answers to all his questions. There was no chance to get either of their votes, so I wanted to waste as little of my brief thirty minutes on them as possible.

Marshall asked me something that was less a question than it was a hint as to how I should argue the case to win—namely, by focusing exclusively on the lower courts' discussion of intent. Nothing else mattered. From that moment on, I skipped everything I had been saying about why *Bolden* should be applied narrowly and directed the justices to every word in the opinions below that could support a finding that the county's at-large elections were intentionally used to discriminate. As I read slowly from parts of the court of appeals opinion, all the justices were fixed on what I was saying. For that matter, the entire courtroom was engrossed; uncharacteristically, there was no hint of whispering among the public who were there to watch the argument.

O'Connor asked two questions that made me think I would get her vote, and as I counted heads in the middle of the argument, I thought I would also get Blackmun and win. It was a heady moment, and standing on the Supreme Court steps after the argument, I felt I had defied the odds and won. When the decision came down, it turned out I was right. I even got Burger, and we won by six votes to three.

I had testified before the House and Senate Subcommittees in 1981 and 1982 that were considering the proposed voting legislation, and a good bill passed the House. But the Senate looked very different. Strom Thurmond had one of the worst records on race of any politician in the last fifty years, and he chaired the Judiciary Committee. Warren Hatch chaired the Subcommittee on the Constitution, and he was extremely conservative on race issues as well. To top it off, Brad Reynolds testified for the Reagan Justice Department against the legislation. But strange politics began to stir that suggested a deal might be possible, and in the end the House bill passed the Senate by a wide margin.

Bolden was gone, and the new amendment to the Voting Rights Act expressly banned any law, practice or procedure that *results* in discrimination. The need to prove intentional discrimination was officially interred. Because the congressional sponsors of the legislation were rightfully skeptical of the Supreme Court, they included an extensive report with the bill in an effort to prevent the court from issuing future rulings that were more restrictive of voting claims than Congress intended. The report explained at length the kinds of practices that were illegal under the new Section 2 results test and how the courts should apply the new law.[28]

The *Bolden* decision was terrible, but Congress had infused new life into the Voting Rights Act. There was reason to be optimistic that the voting rights of *all* Americans might soon be fulfilled and *equal* after 1982. But only time would tell if that optimism was justified.

6

The Bush–Gore Election: A Bloodless Coup

The 2000 presidential race between Al Gore and George W. Bush was supposed to be a contest of ideas, not survival. Gore had made himself the nation's most prominent advocate for tackling climate change. For almost two centuries, scientists had known that carbon dioxide traps heat in the atmosphere, yet Gore's insistence that the United States lead the world toward renewable energy terrified the fossil-fuel industry. Bush became their champion, though by today's standards he seems almost mild—he never stooped to calling global warming a "hoax," for example.

Another issue that seems unthinkable now dominated headlines then: what to do with the federal budget *surplus*. Years of fiscal restraint under Bill Clinton had left Washington awash in revenue. Republicans, led by Bush, wanted tax cuts heavily skewed toward the wealthy; Gore argued for paying down the national debt. The candidates sparred, too, over abortion rights, gun regulation, and the power of insurance companies over medical care.

Those debates were real, but in the end they were irrelevant. What made the election of 2000 infamous was not its policy disputes but its theft. When the polls closed on November 7, the presidency came down to one state—Florida—and what happened there was not a farce but a calculated act of political sabotage. A corrupt voter purge, post-election chaos orchestrated by Republican operatives, and a lawless Supreme Court decision combined to override the will of the people.

From the beginning, the deck was stacked against Gore. Florida's governor, Jeb Bush, was the candidate's brother and as determined as anyone in America to see him win. Florida's chief election officer, Secretary of State Katherine Harris, was not merely partisan—she was a zealot. She co-chaired Bush's Florida campaign, campaigned for him outside the state, and still insisted on supervising the count that would decide who became president. Republicans who prattle endlessly about "public confidence in elections" ignored her glaring conflict of interest.

The theft began months before a single ballot was cast, hidden inside what was sold as an innocuous "good-government" reform. Officials claimed they were cleaning the voter rolls—removing duplicates, the dead, and ineligible felons. In reality it became a purge of lawful Democratic voters. Harris's predecessor, Republican Sandra Mortham, had hired Database Technologies (DBT) to compile the purge list. In early 2000, DBT was absorbed by ChoicePoint, a data-mining company whose board included major Republican donors.

Purging voter rolls can be done with error rates below 1 percent, but accuracy was not what Florida wanted. Harris's Division of Elections ordered DBT to cast a wide net—to "capture more names" *even if they were innocent.* DBT's analysts objected that such methods would create "false positives," wrongly branding thousands of voters as felons. The state's reply was chilling: That's what they wanted, to capture more names even if they weren't matches.[1]

Under Florida's directives, a "match" didn't need to be exact. A partial match—similar spelling, reversed first and last names, different suffixes—was enough to put a voter on the purge list.[2] DBT warned that the instructions "defied logic," but followed orders. The resulting purge list was a masterpiece of misidentification, filled with legitimate voters, disproportionately African American—people most likely to support Gore.

The DBT contract had required manual verification, phone calls, and statistical checks to ensure accuracy. None were done. Florida officials knew what those checks would show—that the list was rotten. One example alone revealed the scale of the fraud: 8,000 Florida voters labeled as Texas felons. None were. They had committed minor misdemeanors and retained full voting rights. The error was caught only because one county supervisor happened to figure it out. How many voters were erased around the state before the error was caught will never be known.

Another layer of injustice compounded the damage. Florida then was one of only four states that required residents convicted of felonies to seek a rare gubernatorial clemency before regaining the right to vote. But 50,000 current Florida residents had been convicted and served their sentences in a state that automatically re-enfranchised them, and the Florida Court of Appeals had ruled that those rights carried over when they moved to Florida. "Once another state restores the civil rights of one of its citizens whose rights had been lost because of a conviction in that state, they are restored and the State of Florida has no authority to suspend or restore them at that point. The matter is simply at an end."[3]

But the matter was far from at an end for Jeb Bush and Katherine Harris. Harris quietly instructed county officials to purge all out-of-state ex-felons anyway. When one county supervisor asked for the illegal order in writing, the governor's Office of Executive Clemency obliged, stating that even those whose rights had been restored elsewhere had to ask Bush for clemency. The directive was not just unlawful—the office later admitted the obvious, that it didn't even have the authority to grant clemency for an out-of-state conviction.[4] Nearly 3,000 properly registered Floridians vanished from the rolls because of the order. Thousands more were blocked from registering at all, wrongly told they were barred.

County election supervisors were horrified when they received the purge lists. In Leon County, officials found that of the 694 names ordered removed, only thirty-four should have been.[5] Previous purge lists had been subject to local verification. This time the state dumped an error-filled database on counties that had neither the staff nor the time to fix it. Some supervisors rebelled and ignored the list altogether. Others, unsure what to do, mailed letters telling targeted voters they had thirty days to prove their innocence by submitting fingerprints or other documents to the state. For many, that bureaucratic gauntlet was impossible. People from states where voting rights were restored automatically were told to provide documentation that didn't exist.

ChoicePoint, for its part, knew the racial composition of those flagged but refused to release that data, calling it a "trade secret." What was no secret was the scale. Tens of thousands were on the purge list. In Miami-Dade County alone, 7,150 names appeared on the list. Of those, 954 were later proven erroneous and reinstated. The remaining 6,200 were a mystery—some actual Florida felons and many who were not were all erased in the confusion.

The purge was invisible to the public until it was too late. On election day, thousands of citizens arrived at their precincts only to learn that, on paper, they no longer existed. The U.S. Civil Rights Commission later concluded that "countless eligible voters were wrongfully turned away from the polls" and that the damage "fell most harshly on the shoulders of black voters."[6] Typical was Sandylynn Williams, a Tampa resident who had never committed a felony in her life. A loyal Gore supporter, she was turned away when her name appeared on the purge list. Ten days *after the election* she received a letter from the county apologizing for the mistake.[7]

Florida was decided by 537 votes. The number of African Americans and other Democrats wrongly purged or prevented from registering exceeded that margin many times over. The presidency, quite literally, turned on the state's willful defiance of the law and its calculated suppression of eligible voters.

And Republicans didn't stop with purging Gore voters—they also disregarded Florida law to *increase* the number of Bush votes. Florida required that absentee ballot applications include the voter's identification number, and applications had to be signed after they were filled out. In Republican Seminole County, over 2,000 thousand absentee applications distributed by the Republican Party did not include the required voter identification number when they were submitted. The county election supervisor's office informed the Republican political director of their problem and invited him to use their office for the next two weeks to change the applications, even though they had already been signed and attested to by the voters under oath.

In the same November 2000 election, Seminole County told a Democratic candidate for the legislature that absentee applications he had solicited would be discarded if they lacked any of the required information. A few months earlier, they rejected another candidate's petition for technical reasons. When he asked for the petition so he could fix it, he was refused and told that once a document was submitted it couldn't be changed.[8] The election office in Martin County went one better than Seminole County when they let a party operative remove hundreds of Republican applications, change them, and then bring them back. While these election officials' help for Bush didn't have the same rank smell as Harris' purge of Democratic voters, they gave Bush about 3,000 additional votes.

When the sun came up on election day, Al Gore didn't know that a lot of Florida's Democratic voters wouldn't be allowed to cast a ballot. Nor could he ever have imagined all that would go wrong on election day itself.

Trouble began in Palm Beach the moment the doors opened. Voters stepped up to the Votomatic punch card machines, followed the arrows on the confusing "butterfly" ballot, and far too many walked away having accidentally voted for Pat Buchanan instead of Al Gore because of the confusing way the candidates' names were laid out on the ballot. Some realized the mistake inside the booth, panicked, and tried to "fix" it by punching a second hole for Gore. That well-intended second punch turned their ballot into an overvote—invalid on its face. By late morning, the confusion had become a chorus. The election supervisor issued "clarifying" instructions to poll workers that read like a riddle: "Remind all voters coming in that they are to vote only for one (1) presidential candidate and that they are to punch the hole next to the arrow next to the number next to the candidate that they wish to vote for."[9] Not only was the clarification anything but clear, many of the county's voters had already cast their ballots—the damage had been done.

Even Buchanan acknowledged what was happening. "When I took one look at that ballot on election night," he said, "it's very easy. . .to see how someone could have voted for me in the belief they voted for Al Gore."[10] The final tally in Palm Beach gave Buchanan 3,407 votes—a political impossibility given the county's demographics and Buchanan's record. He drew votes in a heavily Jewish precinct that included Holocaust survivors who despised him for his past remarks about Hitler and Nazi Germany. Some of those voters were physically sick at the thought that they might have voted for him. The Bush campaign knew the design error had siphoned thousands from Gore, but Bush spokesman Ari Fleischer tried to obfuscate. He told reporters that Palm Beach was a Buchanan "stronghold." Buchanan's own campaign coordinator said that claim was "nonsense."[11]

The miscast Buchanan votes weren't the only blow for Gore. Thousands of overvotes—double-punched Buchanan–Gore ballots—were kicked out by the machines. Buchanan was blunt: if a card showed punches for Buchanan and Gore, "almost certainly those are Al Gore's votes and not mine."[12] In Palm Beach alone, 5,330 of the rejected ballots were exactly that kind of double-punch error.[13]

By Wednesday, November 8, the first statewide returns had Bush up by 1,784 votes out of nearly 6 million cast. Florida law mandated a machine recount when margins were that thin. By Thursday the recount had whittled Bush's edge to 227. What stunned everyone wasn't just the closeness, but that the tabulators failed to read 180,000 ballots—113,000 of which the scanner "saw" as overvotes and 60,000 as undervotes. The presidency was reeling over a vast sea of "no votes."

Later analyses would show that Black voters' ballots were rejected by tabulators at several times the rate of white voters' ballots. The reason wasn't voter error; it was the equipment. In some precincts, usually the more affluent ones, scanners were designed to refuse an overvote and give voters a redo; in others, there was no such safeguard, and rejection rates soared. Poorer counties that were disproportionately minority had equipment that lacked the "overvote failsafe" feature. As a result, they had higher spoilage rates, sometimes above 10 percent. Nearly all of the state's precincts with the worst spoiled-ballot rates were Black-majority.[14] Two things were immediately obvious. The number of machine-rejected ballots dwarfed the margin between the candidates, and a huge share of those rejections came from Democratic strongholds.

By Thursday the Gore camp was under siege. They were behind on the machine count, but if someone would simply *look* at the irregularities and the rejected ballots—if someone would follow the bedrock rule of election law that "the intent of the voter is paramount"—they believed Gore would win. Their task was to get someone in authority to act, and act fast.

The Bush team saw the same landscape and drew the opposite conclusion. Their only path to victory was to stop everyone from examining the ballots. Freeze the total. Run out the clock. Delay and obstruct. And they had a crucial ally: the Florida Secretary of State, Katherine Harris, whose loyalties overrode any sense of fidelity she might have had to fairly administering the election.

Everyone understood the chad problem that came with punch card voting. Chads sometimes didn't detach cleanly, and the scanners would register a "no vote" where a human eye could plainly see the voter's intent. This wasn't a novel issue in Florida in 2000. Around the country, problems with chads were common and had been resolved time and time again by manual recounts. Florida had recently done exactly that in another race.

Election officials had an entire vocabulary for chad failures: hanging chads, swinging-door chads, dimpled chads, and pregnant chads. Veterans of these fights agreed on one point—hand counts were more accurate than machine tallies, and Florida law reflected that reality. If there was "an error in vote tabulation which could affect the outcome," a manual recount was required. County canvassing boards—typically comprised of the county election supervisor, a local judge, and a county commissioner—were required to apply that rule. In most years, their decisions were uncontroversial. This time, passions were white-hot—and Harris stood poised to tilt the scales.

Republicans argued there could be no manual recounts so long as the machines were "working." If a scanner correctly computed that two plus two equals four, they said, nothing more could be done—even if a punch card showed a clear presidential choice that the machine missed. Democrats argued the opposite. If a ballot revealed voter intent but the machine failed to catch it, that is exactly what is meant by an "error in tabulation," and the law mandated a hand count.

On Saturday, November 11, the Palm Beach County canvassing board met to decide Gore's request for a manual recount. Florida's procedure called for an initial 1 percent sample; if that sample showed a significant variance, the board was required to conduct a countywide hand count. Technically, Harris had no formal vote with the canvassing board, but her office's opinions carried weight. Gore's problem was predictable. Harris would say the boards were prohibited from manual recounts—not because the statute said so, but because Bush led. Had the vote count been reversed, she would have read the statute the opposite way.

Harris sent one of her lawyers, Kerey Carpenter, to the meeting. Her mission was clear—don't let anything "untoward" happen, like letting the board determine voter intent by hand. With both campaigns pressing their legal theories, Carpenter took the board chair—Judge Charles Burton—aside and urged him to request a formal opinion from Harris before proceeding. Why Burton agreed is unclear; any letter from Harris would be political to the bone. But before he could act, board member Carol Roberts moved to expand the recount to the entire county based on the substantial differences already seen in the 1 percent sample. Her motion carried, by three votes to two, with Burton smoldering in dissent.

Carpenter's partial failure masked her bigger success. During the initial review of the sample ballots, the board had done what the law, and common sense, required—identified voter intent by examining the chads. By Saturday afternoon it looked like Gore would net enough votes from the 1 percent sample alone to overtake Bush. That shift—small in raw numbers but seismic in narrative—would have transformed the politics, the media framing, and the public's sense of who had truly won Florida.

But it was not to be. Carpenter—the "Chad Whisperer," as history might remember her—again worked her influence on Judge Burton the moment the hand-count began swinging toward Gore. She pressed him to adopt a new, more restrictive standard, one that would ignore clear indications of a voter's intent that the board had recognized moments earlier. Incredibly, Burton told the board to start over and review the ballots under a much more restrictive test. The air went out of the room. Gore still gained votes, but far fewer than the sample alone had first shown.[15] The window was rapidly closing on the Democratic candidate.

Meanwhile, Harris delivered the opinion everyone expected. County boards, she decreed, could not grant Gore's hand-count requests. Still, Bush's camp worried that Palm Beach or another "rogue" board might proceed anyway and flip the numbers. They wanted to shut everything down for good. On Saturday they filed a federal lawsuit against the four counties that were conducting hand recounts (Miami-Dade, Palm Beach, Broward, and Volusia), demanding an injunction to stop them cold.

The legal theory was, to put it kindly, inventive. Bush's lawyers argued that hand recounts violated the Equal Protection Clause because different counties might judge ballots differently. Their logic was upside down. In effect, the Bush team was arguing that it was better to have *more inaccurate* results than *more accurate* ones. "All bad is better than half bad." It was the kind of logic that would make every state's recount law unconstitutional—and it collided with the uncontested fact that hand counts were more accurate than punch-card counting machines. Even worse for Bush, as governor of Texas he had just signed a statute endorsing liberal manual recounts.

On Monday, two days after Bush's case was filed, U.S. District Judge Donald Middlebrooks made his ruling. Florida's recount system, he wrote, fully complied with Supreme Court precedent.[16] The hand-count provision "strives to strengthen rather than dilute the right to vote by securing, as nearly as humanly possible, an accurate and true reflection of the will of the electorate." As for Bush's complaint about differing standards among counties, Middlebrooks pointed out that local variation had always been part of elections in the United States. Unless all 3,142 counties and parishes in the United States used the exact same system, variation was inevitable.

But frivolous claims can be strategic ones. The Bush team's backup plan was to reach out to the U.S. Supreme Court if need be, whose seven Republican justices might deliver what Florida's voters would not. Their case might have looked frivolous, but it had one strategic purpose: to inject a federal issue into the record, a thread they could later pull on to reach the U.S. Supreme Court.

A week had passed since election day, and the nation was transfixed. The rest of the world was incredulous. *Le Monde*'s headline read, "A Banana Republic." Other European papers expressed open disbelief that the world's leading democracy couldn't count its own votes. The *Guardian* called the spectacle "a circus of chaos." In India, newspapers offered to send election monitors to show America how to hold an honest election.

Inside both campaigns, no one was sleeping. For Gore's team, time was the enemy; for Bush's, it was the ally. Every hour that ticked by hardened the machine total that put Bush ahead. Then, on the same day that Middlebrooks issued his ruling, Harris dropped her next bombshell. She announced that she would certify the election the very next day, November 14, and that no votes counted after that moment would be included. Her opinion letter dismissing manual recounts was still warm when she set the deadline. Palm Beach halted its count in confusion. Broward County did the opposite—defying Harris and voting to proceed manually. Volusia County had already finished a recount, narrowing Bush's lead but not enough to put Gore ahead.

That same day, Florida Attorney General Bob Butterworth issued a formal opinion contradicting Harris. An "error in tabulation," he said, plainly included a machine's failure to read a ballot when voter intent was clear. Butterworth, an elected Democrat outside Jeb Bush's circle of control, gave Gore's side a legal foothold—but not enough to stop Harris.

Soon afterwards, Circuit Judge Terry Lewis ruled that Harris had acted arbitrarily by refusing to accept the late returns from Broward and Miami-Dade. He ordered her to reconsider. Harris responded the very next day, rejecting the late returns once again, but this time sprinkling her letters with boilerplate legalisms. When the plaintiffs returned to Lewis expecting enforcement of his earlier order, he stunned them by calling Harris' latest ruling an "exercise of reasoned judgment." Substance had lost to form. Bush partisans erupted in cheers; Gore's lawyers stood speechless. The machinery of obstruction had done its job.

Just as both sides were adjusting to Judge Lewis's latest order, the Florida Supreme Court detonated a bomb. Two hours after Republicans had been celebrating, the court abruptly intervened—expediting Gore's appeal, consolidating it with the Volusia County Canvassing Board's case, and setting oral argument for Monday, November 20. The speed alone startled some observers, but what truly rattled Bush's team was the court's injunction forbidding Katherine Harris from certifying the presidential election "until further order." Gore's lawyers hadn't even asked for that relief. The justices had granted it of their own volition—preserving the status quo, the cardinal rule of equity that every law student knows.

The Monday argument became global theater. Cameras carried it live; nearly a hundred lawyers had filed briefs, but the spotlight fell on the Republicans' lead counsel, Michael Carvin, a forty-three-year-old lawyer who had been in the Reagan Justice Department and built a career representing conservative causes. Carvin was personable outside the courtroom but a ferocious appellate lawyer who went on to argue landmark cases that gutted the Voting Rights Act—but this wasn't his day. The justices peppered him relentlessly. "Isn't the intent of the voter what we need to focus on, Mr. Carvin?" one asked, and the packed courtroom could feel the tide turning.

The next afternoon the Florida Supreme Court delivered a unanimous opinion declaring Harris's actions illegal. Her partisan defiance had stripped her of the deference normally owed to public officials. Parsing the Florida election code line by line, the justices ruled that Harris must accept recount returns until 5 p.m. Sunday, November 26—effectively restoring the five days her obstruction had cost. Manual recounts would continue. For Gore, it was oxygen; for Bush, an alarm.

Having lost in both state and federal courts, Bush's strategists went to war on every front. They petitioned the U.S. Supreme Court to review Florida's decision. There was no automatic right of appeal, but the Republican-dominated Supreme Court might give Bush a hearing, even though nothing had happened that was inconsistent with the court's election precedents. Meanwhile, on the ground, Bush launched a street campaign. The marching order was blunt: "Shut down the recounts."

At the Miami-Dade Canvassing Board, Republican operatives packed the hall, pounding on tables, shouting, and shoving officials. Television crews were knocked to the floor. A Democratic lawyer was dragged to safety as the crowd shouted that he was stealing ballots. In fact, he had a blank sample ballot. The orchestrated riot—later dubbed the Brooks Brothers Riot because many participants were Capitol Hill staffers dressed in office attire—succeeded where legal briefs had failed. The terrified board halted its hand count. It was open, televised election interference, but no arrests were made, and the Bush team had stopped 10,000 ballots that the machine scanner couldn't read from being counted.

By Saturday, November 25, Broward County had finished its recount, adding 567 votes to Gore's total. Palm Beach, still sorting through thousands of disputed ballots, pleaded for more time. Harris refused and certified Bush the victor by 537 votes. Had Palm Beach been allowed to finish—and had Judge Burton not buckled under Carpenter's pressure to change standards—Gore would have won Florida.

To most observers, that seemed the end. Yet paradoxically, Harris's certification was what Gore needed to be able to file an election contest in state court, and on Monday, November 27, he did exactly that.

But trouble was brewing far beyond Tallahassee. In Washington, the U.S. Supreme Court agreed to fast-track Bush's appeal, scheduling a hearing for Friday, December 1. Bush's lawyers argued that only the Florida Legislature, not its courts, could determine how the state's electoral votes were allocated—and that the Florida Supreme Court had usurped legislative power by extending the recount deadline. It was a flimsy claim, but with seven Republican appointees on the U.S. Supreme Court, "flimsy" might still win.

When the arguments opened, Chief Justice William Rehnquist could barely conceal his intent to hand the presidency to Bush. Yet other justices' questions suggested doubt. Some seemed unconvinced by the tortured logic that state courts couldn't interpret their own laws. Gore's legal team left cautiously optimistic.

However, their optimism didn't last. On December 4, the trial judge in Gore's election contest ruled against him. That same day, the U.S. Supreme Court issued a strange, unanimous order instructing the Florida Supreme Court to "clarify" its prior opinion—an opinion that was perfectly clear and needed no "clarification." The real motive was internal politics. The court's more extreme conservatives hoped Florida's clarification might bolster the argument that the state court had violated federal law; the moderates hoped for the opposite.

From that point, the pace was dizzying. On Thursday, December 7, the Florida Supreme Court again heard arguments—this time on Gore's appeal in the election contest—and the very next day ordered a statewide recount of every ballot the machines had recorded as "no vote." Palm Beach's hand-counted ballots that Harris had rejected were to be included; Miami-Dade's halted recount was to resume. Everything pointed to a coming Gore victory once those votes were tallied.

Then, in a move that stunned even veteran court watchers, the U.S. Supreme Court intervened again on December 9. Without briefing, without oral argument, and without precedent, it ordered all recounts stopped—immediately. The vote was five to four.

Justice Antonin Scalia issued an astounding separate opinion. The count had to be halted, he said, to prevent "casting a cloud upon what [Bush] claims to be the legitimacy of his election." The logic was surreal. Counting all the votes, Scalia acknowledged, might reveal that Gore had won, which would indeed "cast a cloud" on Bush's claim to victory. But that wasn't an outcome Scalia was willing to permit. The manual count had to stop so Gore couldn't pull ahead.

Five justices had just picked a president. Gore won 350,000 more votes than Bush nationally, but he lacked the one vote he needed to win the election—the vote of one of the five Republican justices who anointed Bush.

The U.S. Supreme Court issued its final opinion on December 12, and there were no surprises. It was devoid of legal justification and sits alone in the law books as an ugly political charade. The justices effectively admitted their decision was lawless when they wrote, "Our consideration is limited to the present circumstances." Of course it was. There was no law to back it up, it was based on no legal principles, and it was inconsistent with everything the court—and the conservative justices in particular—had ever said about election law. You didn't have to be a constitutional scholar or a lawyer with Supreme Court experience to know that the case was decided based on the political parties of the candidates.

The majority tried to justify the indefensible by saying there wasn't enough time left to complete a proper recount. That was laughable. The Florida Supreme Court had established a procedure to ensure that time was not a problem. Populous Leon County had completed its manual count in twelve hours. The decision wasn't about time—it was about making sure Bush was the 43rd president. As Republican Justice David Souter wrote in dissent, "There is no justification for denying the State the opportunity to try to count all disputed ballots now."

The ramifications of the stolen presidential election of 2000 have rippled through history, shaping the country and the world in ways that will be debated for generations. But one thing is certain. That election shattered the myth of American democracy's invulnerability and exposed how even a presidential election can be stolen more than a century after the Tilden–Hayes contest. With the starkly political decisions of today's Supreme Court, unfortunately there is no hope for an impartial decision if a presidential election lands there again. As Justice Breyer said in his dissent in *Bush vs. Gore*:

> Although we may never know with complete certainty the identity of the winner of this year's Presidential election, the identity of the loser is perfectly clear. It is the Nation's confidence in the judge as an impartial guardian of the rule of law.

7

Drawing Districts to Win and Screw the Other Guy

A time-honored way to rig elections is by drawing districts to elect who you want and squeeze out who you don't want. It sounds preposterous today, but for 180 years elections in the U.S. were run using malapportioned districts that gave "preferred voters" *ten or even a hundred times* more political power than anyone else.

The most contentious issue at the Constitutional Convention was representation in the new Congress. Some delegates wanted representation to be based on population, others wanted equal representation allocated to the states, regardless of population, since the new country was in theory a federal union of states of equal political status. The compromise that enabled the creation of the United States incorporated both ideas, the House of Representatives based on population and the Senate where all states had the same two votes regardless of their population.

Representation by population in the House is mandated by Article 1, Section 2. It requires that the seats in Congress be reapportioned to the states after every census. But what about the legislatures of the states? The Constitution required states to have a Republican Form of Government, but it was silent as to how the states should establish districts for their legislatures. That was originally left to the states to do as they chose.

When the country was new, transportation and communication were extremely slow. It made some sense in creating districts for state legislatures to base them on towns and counties since the people in those communities shared much of the same general interests, a universal one being improving transportation. But during the 1800s, demands for districts based on population became more insistent. The fact that the House of Representatives was based on population supported the argument for population-based state legislatures, and that took on more weight when Congress passed the Apportionment Act of 1872. For the first time, beginning with the 1870 census, Congress required that each state's congressional districts contain "as nearly as practicable an equal number of inhabitants." That requirement was contained in each subsequent reapportionment until Congress passed the permanent Reapportionment Act of 1929 that turned reapportionment determinations over to the Census Bureau.

The impetus for equalizing state legislative districts continued to grow as population shifted. Industrialization drew people to the cities while the population of many rural areas stagnated or even decreased. By the middle of the nineteenth century, the elimination of property ownership requirements also added more voters in urban areas than in rural ones, which exacerbated the overweighting of rural votes.

Arguments against population equality were mostly just sham pretexts to justify entrenched political power. Legislators sometimes said frequent rebalancing was too complicated. While redistricting is politically fractious, that was no excuse for failing to do it. Sometimes lawmakers were candid that they opposed redistricting to avoid giving power to the cities. The Supreme Court even said that discriminating against urban voters in favor of a state's "thinly populated counties" was justifiable because people in urban counties had "practical opportunities for exerting their political weight at the polls not available to [rural voters]."[1] In truth, though, the refusal to fairly district state legislatures largely boiled down to the fact that legislators did not want to change the districts they were elected from. New districts were a personal threat.

There were compromises in some states that modeled their legislatures on Congress—one chamber population-based with redistricting every census, and another comprised of some combination of counties regardless of their population. While that system was an improvement in theory, it made little difference in practice because state legislatures usually ignored the requirement that they redistrict.

As the twentieth century progressed, the country continued to urbanize while districts remained frozen. It was obvious that a legislative solution was out of reach; a judicial remedy was the only hope for reform. The first Supreme Court case where malapportioned districts were challenged was *Colegrove vs. Green* in 1946, and it was a big disappointment.[2] The opinion in *Colegrove* was written by Felix Frankfurter, who wrote that it would be "undemocratic" to "involve the judiciary in the politics of the people"—strange logic since the problem was the *absence* of democracy. Go to the legislature for a remedy, Frankfurter wrote, even though he knew that was impossible.

Hugo Black wrote a dissenting opinion that scoffed at Frankfurter's idea that the "proper remedy" was political. "Such a gross inequality in the voting power of citizens irrefutably demonstrates a complete lack of effort [by the legislature] to make an equitable apportionment." Justice Black pointed out that everyone would agree that it was unconstitutional to completely deny the right to vote to people who lived in one area of the state. Why should it be any different, he asked, where they are given only a small fraction of the vote allocated to people elsewhere? Frankfurter had no answer to that.

Malapportionment after the *Colegrove* case got progressively worse. City populations increased and suburban populations expanded rapidly after World War II. At the same time the stagnation and decline of rural populations continued, so that staggering disparities were now the norm across the country.

In California, Los Angeles County, with its six million residents in 1960, had one state senator. A sparsely populated district in the Sierra Nevada mountains also had one senator, giving a single voter there over a hundred times the influence of voters in Los Angeles. Alabama voters from the least populous county had forty-one times the clout of a voter from the most populous county in electing state senators and sixteen times more in the House. But the South looked progressive compared to Connecticut, where Hartford had two state representatives for its 162,000 residents and Union also had two representatives for its 400 residents, a whopping disparity of 405:1.[3] New Hampshire, not to be outdone by its New England neighbor, hadn't redistricted in a very long time and people were subjected to—or enjoyed, depending on where you lived—a voting disparity of 1,081:1.[4] Georgia "only" gave a 99:1 advantage to the most rural county compared to the most populous Atlanta county, but Georgia also had its unique county-unit system that locked in rural control for statewide races.

The house of cards finally came crashing down in 1962 with the Supreme Court's decision in *Baker v. Carr*[5] that relegated *Colegrove* to the trash bin with other shameful decisions. *Baker* caused a seismic shift in American democracy, redistributing power across the nation and rewriting the rules of political engagement. After he retired, Earl Warren said *Baker* was the court's most important decision while he was Chief Justice, even more so than *Brown v. Board of Education*.[6]

Lore developed around the *Baker* case that it killed one justice and put another in the hospital. That story was rooted in the fact that Justice Frankfurter, who was livid over his *Colegrove* opinion being reversed, suffered a stroke and had to retire from the court. Justice Whittaker was way out of his depth on the court and often voted with whichever justice spoke to him last. He vacillated daily while *Baker* was pending and finally retired with a nervous breakdown just days after the Supreme Court issued the *Baker* decision.

Congressional districts had a strange history. By the middle of the nineteenth century, six of the states that had more than one representative elected them all statewide without districts. In those states, one party typically had a solid majority of the statewide vote so that at-large elections gave that party the entire congressional delegation. Even a 40–45 percent minority was shut out. That changed with the Apportionment Act of 1842, which for the first time required that representatives be elected from single-member districts. But congressional malapportionment reigned until equal population districts were mandated by Congress in 1872, a requirement that unfortunately lapsed in 1929. By the time *Baker* was decided, congressional districts within some states varied by 3:1 and 4:1. That was stopped two years after *Baker* when the Supreme Court ruled that a state's congressional districts also had to be equalized.[7]

While we take one-person, one-vote for granted today, malapportionment isn't some relic of a distant past—it's a stark reminder of how fragile democracy can be. It's especially important today to remember that equality in representation would never have become the law of the land were it not for the brief time when the Supreme Court breathed life into the Constitution under Earl Warren's leadership.

You can be sure that today's Supreme Court wouldn't require equal population districts if it weren't already so entrenched in people's minds. You can see that in post-*Baker* cases. For some years after *Baker*, the court went on to apply the equal population rule to county commissions, school boards, and other government entities, but in 1973 the new conservative justices brought an abrupt halt to that trend. Justice Rehnquist wrote the opinion in that case, upholding a state law that allowed landowners—including corporations that owned land—to vote for public water district commissioners *based on the number of acres they owned.* It was malapportionment in the extreme.[8] And that wasn't all the Supreme Court condoned in that case. Justice Black wrote a dissenting opinion for himself and the other two remaining members of the court who believed the right to vote should be *equal* and for *people*:

> The vices of this case are fourfold. First. Lessees of farmlands, though residents of the district, are not given the franchise. Second. Residents who own no agricultural lands but live in the district and face all the perils of flood which the district is supposed to control are disfranchised. Third. Only agricultural landowners are entitled to vote, and their vote is weighted, one vote for each one hundred dollars of assessed valuation. *Fourth. The corporate voter is put in the saddle* [italics added].

Rehnquist would surely have voted with Frankfurter had he been on the Supreme Court when *Baker* was decided. The same is true for the other Republican justices on the court today. If they had had first crack at the issue, we wouldn't have a one-person, one-vote rule today.

Malapportionment was a powerful form of gerrymandering, but it isn't the way most people today think of a gerrymander. Instead, they think of a district, usually but not always strangely shaped, that was drawn to give an advantage to one person, one racial group, or, most commonly, one political party. Gerrymandering is as old as the republic. It's the ultimate political game of rigging elections before voters cast their ballots.

The term dates back to 1812 when Massachusetts Governor Elbridge Gerry approved a contorted districting plan for the State Senate that benefited his Democratic-Republican Party at the expense of the Federalists. When an artist drew a cartoon caricaturing the district as a serpent, someone commented, "That looks like a salamander," but another responded, "No, that's a Gerrymander."[9] From then on, "gerrymandering" has meant drawing districts to secure power. The Gerry cartoon, shown on the next page, is a classic.

Over the years, gerrymandering has produced famously absurd districts. Illinois gave us the "Bullwinkle" and "Earmuff" districts, Pennsylvania the cartoonish "Goofy Kicking Donald Duck District," and Ohio the "Lake Erie Monster." Gerrymandering is a pernicious threat to fair elections, and, especially in the South, gerrymanders have been rooted in racism for 150 years.

Mississippi's Shoestring District was drawn in the 1870s to corral most of the state's Black voters into that one district, leaving the other six districts safely in white control.[10]

Georgia's Fifth Congressional District was the prototype for racial gerrymandering in more recent times. Atlanta and Fulton County have long been home to Black businesses, authors, colleges, and political leaders, and the home to the biggest concentration of Black voters in the state. To neutralize those voters, Fulton County was paired with two very white, conservative rural counties, and winning the most votes didn't matter. Again exploiting Georgia's county-unit system, victory was determined not by winning the popular vote, but by winning the most county units, and the two conservative white counties combined were allocated more unit votes than Fulton, even though they had a far smaller population. That gerrymander left Atlanta and its Black voters represented for years by a congressman who was a favorite of the Ku Klux Klan.

After the Supreme Court struck down county-unit voting in the 1960s, Georgia's mapmakers drew the Fifth District to exclude by a single block the residences of prominent Black political leaders who would have been strong congressional candidates.[11] The state just couldn't shake its worst instincts when the next redistricting came around after the 1980 census. The General Assembly drew a Fifth District that was better than before but balked at giving a Black candidate "too good" a chance to win, even though the Fifth District was the only district out of Georgia's ten districts where a Black candidate had any chance.

I represented the Legislative Black Caucus in challenging that plan, and it looked at the outset like it would be a tough case given the Supreme Court's growing hostility to voting rights. But the case turned in our favor when several white legislators testified that the chairman of the House Reapportionment Committee had said many times that he wouldn't permit a more favorable district for Black candidates because "I don't want to draw nigger districts."[12] I'm sure the right-wing justices on the Supreme Court didn't like the fact that we won in the trial court, but the racist evidence was too hot for them to handle. They affirmed the lower court decision without writing an opinion.

Southern racial gerrymandering morphed into political gerrymandering as Republicans captured Southern legislatures. Since African Americans were predominantly Democrats, Republicans drew a few districts with very high Black percentages. By packing districts with Black Democratic voters, Republicans were able to control a disproportionate share of all the other districts. Justice Scalia acknowledged exactly that fact in another case I argued in the Supreme Court, saying that "It's been in the interest of a particular political party on occasion to put all the Black voters in one district so that all the other districts can go to the other party."[13]

There has been a well-deserved uproar over Trump's demand that Texas and other red states revise their congressional districts mid-census to further gerrymander their plans. Politically driven mid-census redistricting by Republicans is not new, though. As they took over Southern legislatures, Republicans didn't wait until the next census to strengthen their hand. Georgia was once again a sordid example. When Republicans won a majority of the legislature in the 2004 election, their first order of business in the new session in 2005 was to redistrict to increase their advantage in the General Assembly.

Then they focused on the two remaining white Democratic congressmen in the South, Jim Marshall and John Barrow, by gerrymandering their districts to make them more Republican. Barrow proved a harder target than expected. Republicans first moved his hometown into a reconfigured Republican district, but that gerrymander failed when Barrow moved to Savannah, which was in his old district, and won re-election. The Georgia General Assembly again targeted him and redrew his district in 2012 so that it was much more Republican. Barrow was finally beaten, and the Republicans' annihilation of white southern congressional Democrats was complete.

Partisan gerrymandering is an obvious corruption of the rights of voters and offends people in both parties, but it has been reviled especially by Democrats since they have been most often on the losing end. For the first time, in a 1986 case, a majority of the Supreme Court acknowledged that excessive political gerrymandering violated the Constitution but left open what evidence was needed to prove districts were so partisan that they were unconstitutional.[14] Three decades passed without the court answering that question, and finally what glimmer of hope existed for judicial relief was snuffed out in 2019.[15]

The opinion in that 2019 case was written by Roberts for the five-Republican majority. Gerrymander claims were deemed "nonjusticiable" in an opinion that borrowed from Frankfurter's seventy-three-year-old *Colegrove* opinion that had been overruled by *Baker vs. Carr*. Roberts tried to justify the ruling by saying there was no objective standard for determining what was a bad enough gerrymander to make it unconstitutional, but this ignored state courts that had successfully decided gerrymander cases under state laws. Roberts' opinion was nothing more than old verbiage retrieved from the dead case cemetery to justify the result he wanted to achieve.

While gerrymandering has always been a method of control, today it is more sophisticated, aggressive, and insidious than in the past. Until the 1960s, redistricting was relatively crude, done mostly with city and county boundaries and census tract lines, but the 1990s brought an explosion of technology and data that allowed mapmakers to manipulate districts much more precisely. Maps have been carefully drawn to pack opposition voters into a few districts or disperse them into multiple districts, rendering them powerless and giving the party that drew the lines more districts than they would win if districting were politically neutral.

Redistricting after the 2010 census was such a banner year for partisan gerrymandering it became known as "The Great Gerrymander of 2012."[16] Republicans were intent on grabbing as much political power as they could, and they used all the tools to design politically optimal plans. The plans that were passed were so biased that Democrats would have to receive *8 percent more votes* than Republicans nationwide in 2012—54 percent to 46 percent—to win a majority of the seats in Congress.

The technicians who drew the maps were right on the money. In the 2012 election, Republicans won a thirty-three-seat advantage while *losing* by 1,400,000 votes. In 2014, Republicans won a fifty-nine-seat advantage with 52.9 percent of the vote, less than Democrats would need to break even, and in 2016, Republicans won a forty-seven-seat majority while winning only 50.5 percent of the national votes cast in congressional races.

Democrats retook the House in 2018, but they received *10 million more* votes than their Republican opponents, and the effect of the 2012 gerrymander had been reduced to some extent by court decisions in Florida, Virginia, and

Pennsylvania that invalidated congressional maps. The lasting power of the Republican gerrymanders was shown by the fact that—in spite of the huge Democratic vote win that year—no incumbent Republican representatives lost to a Democrat in five of the gerrymandered states: Ohio, Missouri, Indiana, Wisconsin, and Tennessee. In North Carolina, where Democratic and Republican voters are close to evenly split, Republicans held ten congressional seats before the 2018 election thanks to extreme gerrymandering and lost only one of them in that election. In the 2020 election, Democrats held on to a small House majority, but, again, they won nearly 5 million more votes than the Republican candidates.

Republican bias in redistricting state legislatures was similar. On average for all states combined, the districts were drawn so that Republicans would win almost 10 percent more seats than Democrats who received the same vote share.[17]

The Republican bias in congressional plans was still very much alive after redistricting in response to the 2020 census. Both Texas and Florida each enacted plans that give Republicans five more congressional seats than they would expect in a fair plan. Gerrymandered plans in four other states (Georgia, North Carolina, Ohio, and Iowa) each give Republicans two additional seats, and five other states (Tennessee, South Carolina, Michigan, Indiana, and Utah) each give one additional seat to Republicans. Offsetting those twenty-three seats were seven seats in states where redistricting plans gave Democrats an advantage.[18] In sum, Republicans started off with a net advantage of sixteen congressional seats before a single vote was cast.

The most notorious effort by Republicans to further gerrymander their maps before the 2026 midterm election has been in Texas. The saga there is not only extraordinary because of the extent of the gerrymander that Republicans want, picking up five more seats in an already badly gerrymandered plan, but because of the unprecedented misuse of federal law enforcement power in that purely political fight. Some Democratic legislators left the state to prevent a quorum and thereby block passage of redistricting legislation. The FBI was directed to track down those legislators, arrest them, and have them returned to Texas to forcibly create a quorum. Using federal law enforcement agents to facilitate a purely political objective of the White House is illegal. It also shows how far Trump will go to steal elections now that the FBI director will do whatever the president wants.

Texas won't be the only state where the gerrymander war of 2026 plays out. Florida, Missouri, Indiana, Ohio, and North Carolina are other states where Republicans are trying to increase their advantage, and they are trying to hang on to the advantage they have in Utah in spite of rulings by the Utah Supreme Court.[19] Naturally, Democrats have responded in kind. California has gerrymandered its congressional map to counteract Texas, and the state's voters approved overriding California's non-partisan Redistricting Commission to do so. Plaintiffs in New York successfully challenged its 11th congressional district in a New York state court, rather than a federal court, that should have prevented the Supreme Court from interfering precipitously. But the court ignored dozens of precedents and blocked the state court order. As Justice Sotomayer wrote in dissent, once again the court had acted as if there were "Rules for thee, but not for me."[20] Democrats also sought favorable redistricting legislation in Virginia and Maryland.

Where the country will be on election day, November 3, 2026, will depend on the final actions of nearly ten states and what the courts do. The new Texas plan was initially enjoined by the trial court because it discriminates racially, but it will still be used because the Supreme Court stayed that injunction and let the new plan go into effect.[21]

Political gerrymandering in the United States is a fundamental perversion of electoral politics. It has always been a way to take political representation from some voters and give it to others, to elect people who otherwise would lose, and to prevent the election of candidates who the voters would choose if plans were fair. Gerrymandering causes major changes in government policies when it flips the party in control, and it aggravates polarization because partisan-optimized districts leave few competitive seats. But as bad as gerrymandering has been historically, it has sunk to new lows with Trump's demand that Republican-controlled state legislatures increase their congressional gerrymanders.

One naturally wonders if gerrymandering could ever be worse, and unfortunately the answer is "yes." Software advances and increased access to data have expanded politicians' ability to manufacture districts to their advantage, and sophisticated AI will soon make those efforts look primitive. The ability of AI to extract information, patterns, and connections from massive amounts of data will make gerrymandering even more powerful. Just as "knowledge is power," information is political power.

Redistricting combines precincts into a district using past election returns from those precincts to predict the likely future partisan vote share for the entire district. No election data exists below the precinct level, but there is a tremendous amount of more granular data that can be used with AI to redistrict more precisely. Some of that data is direct, like census data, and some is modeled to the block level from American Community Survey data. There is also a staggering amount of information for sale from data brokers that is geocoded to individual houses (subscriptions, religion, credit profile, buying patterns, etc.) and can be aggregated to predict block-level voting patterns. AI can assimilate these massive amounts of data and assign voting "values" to every house, combine them into blocks, and combine those blocks into districts with predicted partisan behavior. Districts can also be created with AI to favor or cancel out voter preferences on specific issues.

If mid-census redistricting becomes the norm, districts can also be adjusted regularly to reflect changing demographics and changing issues. AI won't need additional election returns to do that. Gerrymandering may become so refined that voters are rendered little more than data points in an AI-driven game of political chess that is fought out for control.

As long as there's a Republican majority on the Supreme Court, it's unlikely there will be any federal judicial limits to partisan gerrymandering. There have been some good decisions from state courts applying state constitutional provisions to limit gerrymandering, but that remedy will be successful only if the judges involved are fair, which is far from certain. In one case I tried, Georgia's 2002 General Assembly and congressional redistricting plans complied with all of the Supreme Court's requirements, but they favored Democrats. The plans were legal in every respect, but the case flipped from a clear winner to a loser when two very Republican judges were assigned to hear it (the trial was before a three-judge court). It was obvious before they had heard a word of evidence how they intended to rule. They were going to replace Georgia's plans with new ones that were much more friendly to Republicans—so friendly, in fact, that the General Assembly became Republican in the next election for the first time in over a century.

My skepticism about the judiciary keeping partisan gerrymandering at bay is reinforced by some recent state court decisions. In 2022, the North Carolina Supreme Court, which had a majority of Democratic justices, issued a four-to-three decision invalidating the Republican redistricting plans because they were obvious gerrymanders. Then, in the 2022 election, two seats on the court that were previously held by Democrats were won by Republicans. The new Republican majority on the court immediately reversed the prior decision and ordered North Carolina's gerrymandered plans reinstated.[22]

In a 2010 referendum, Florida voters added the Fair Districts Amendment to the state constitution, prohibiting "drawing a plan or district with the intent to favor or disfavor a political party or incumbent." That looks like a strong law, and it was enforced in 2015 when the Florida Supreme Court struck down the state's congressional plan because it was "tainted" by an "unconstitutional intent to favor the Republican Party and incumbent lawmakers."[23]

Florida's purge of partisan manipulation didn't last long, however. After 2020, Governor DeSantis pushed through a new congressional map that the trial court found was unconstitutional but the Florida Supreme Court, now brimming with DeSantis appointees, backed away from its earlier decision and approved the new map.[24] Given that Florida has some of the most partisan maps in the country, the DeSantis judges seem to have effectively "repealed" the state's Fair Districts Amendment.

Ohio's story was similar, and the election for a seat on the Wisconsin Supreme Court in April of 2025 cost over $100 million, mostly money poured in because the election would determine whether Wisconsin's maps—which had already been ruled unconstitutional—would be revived. Elon Musk alone tried to buy the open seat on the court by spending more than $25 million to support the candidate who would uphold the Republican gerrymanders.

With judicial protection from partisan districts sporadic and unreliable, is it possible Congress might act? In 2021, Democrats introduced the Freedom to Vote Act (FVA) that included a mechanism for limiting congressional gerrymanders. An excellent feature of the bill is its use of an objective, statistical way to determine whether a plan should be considered a partisan gerrymander. It also required that cases be fast-tracked and that relief be prompt.

The FVA passed the House in 2022 on a near party-line vote of 220–210 but was blocked by a Republican filibuster in the Senate. The FVA would have done a lot more than just limit gerrymanders, however, such as making voting and voter registration simpler and more accessible, the kinds of reforms that terrify Republican legislators. Maybe an anti-gerrymander law standing alone could one day pass Congress if everyone, Republicans and Democrats alike, get angry enough.

The first independent citizen redistricting commission was established in Arizona in 2000, followed by California in 2010, and both Michigan and Colorado in 2018. Bipartisan, hybrid commissions whose members are largely appointed by party leaders but still function outside the legislature have existed in a few states (Hawaii, Montana, Idaho, Washington, and New Jersey) since the 1970s. Other variants have been added recently in Virginia, New York, and Utah, with mixed success. Maps in all three of those states ended up in litigation.

Commissions can reduce partisan bias and increase competitiveness, but they are no panacea. Ohio's nominally bipartisan redistricting commission has adopted a new plan for 2026 that further gerrymanders the state's congressional districts.[25] Even if there are excellent commissioners drawing a state's maps, there is no obvious answer to the fundamental question of *how* districts should be drawn. Political scientists have offered dozens of suggestions and so have legislators, political parties, community activists, and experienced map drawers. The only thing that is clear is that there is no one right or ideal way to draw districts. Even with a set of principles, specific circumstances will sometimes warrant exceptions.

The country's experience with commission redistricting is so limited that there is little basis for informed opinions beyond what common sense and general experience would already say. Should politicians be completely eliminated from the process? Or should they at least have input into the commission? Possibly there should be legislative members on the commission so long as the decision-making procedure avoids legislative control. A combined system in which a commission works with a legislative committee is a possibility so long as the final authority clearly rests outside the legislature.

Many people latch onto geometric "compactness" as the measure of a good plan, but that misses the point of districting. As the Supreme Court wrote in *Reynolds vs. Sims*,[26] one of the seminal one-person, one-vote cases, "Legislators represent people, not trees or acres. Legislators are elected by voters, not farms or cities or economic interests." Neither do they represent circles, squares, or counties, and the obsession by many with tidy, "pretty-looking" districts is badly misplaced. A district shouldn't be so scattered or irregular that it becomes dysfunctional, but there are many considerations about voter representation in districting that are much more important than what the lines look like or how geometrically compact a district is.

Lastly, should criteria be as absolute as Florida's are written (albeit, not enforced)? Should incumbency be absolutely excluded as a consideration? What if there is an exceptional member of the legislature whose continued service would clearly benefit everyone? Should it be illegal to consider *any* partisan fact? Would it be good alternatively to mandate partisan fairness?

There is no doubt that gerrymandering corrupts our political system in many ways, and it is getting much, much worse. Every two years, there are probably more congressional seats *stolen by gerrymandering* than have ever been stolen in the entire history of the country by someone stuffing ballot boxes in a congressional race. The power to select our representatives needs to be returned to the voters and removed from self-interested incumbents and political parties that want an advantage they don't deserve. Gerrymandering needs stopped either by legislation or the courts. The alternative we're living through now is far too destructive to continue.

8

Stop the Steal!

Stop the Steal! The phrase ricocheted through the streets, across social media, and on every news channel after the 2020 presidential election. Nowhere was it louder or more piercing than in battleground states where passions ran wild. But in the end, the steal that was stopped wasn't the one Trump's devotees had in mind. The real steal—the attempted theft of democracy by Trump and his MAGA followers—*was* stopped.

Nothing like the 2020 election had ever happened before, and the strangest thing about it was that Trump did it in the open. There were secret meetings and conversations, of course, but unlike stuffed ballot boxes in the past, he got as far as he did by *publicly* convincing millions of people that the election had been stolen *from him*. He demanded that his millions of followers pressure state and local officials to overturn the election, and many of the people who descended on the Capitol on January 6, 2021, were so deceived by him that they thought they were righting a wrong by responding to the president's call for an insurrection. As one rioter later testified:

> I was in Washington, D.C. on January 6, 2021, because I believed I was following the instructions of former President Trump and he was my president and the commander-in-chief. [He] had me believing the election was stolen from him.[1]

Innumerable others thought the same thing; they fell for Trump's lies.

The story behind Trump's failed effort to subvert the 2020 presidential election is chilling. Understanding how it happened, and could happen again, starts with a question—who and what is Donald Trump? Much has been written about the kind of person Trump is, and some of the most telling descriptions come from the people who worked with him in his first term as president. They are people that *he chose* to serve in the cabinet and the White House.

They uniformly portray a man who is devoid of empathy for others, who craves personal power and attention, and who has little understanding of national much less global issues. He's obsessed about his coverage on television and social media. He doesn't read, which is unsurprising since he has no concern for the truth. For Trump, "facts" are mere conveniences to be made up to serve his purpose. Mark Esper, Trump's second Secretary of Defense, said in a CNN interview:

> Any elected leader needs to meet some basic criteria: They need to be able to put country over self, they need to have a certain amount of integrity and principle, and they need to be able to reach across the aisle and bring people together and unite the country. Donald Trump doesn't meet [any of] those marks for me.[2]

John Kelly, the White House Chief of Staff, described Trump as "the most flawed person I have ever met," someone whose "dishonesty is astounding."[3]

Trump appointed James Mattis as his first Secretary of Defense partly because he was taken by Mattis' nickname, "Mad Dog," which projected the kind of tough-guy image that Trump desperately wants for himself. Like others, Mattis criticized Trump for "trying to divide us" as a nation. John Bolton, Trump's national security advisor, said Trump was not "fit for office," didn't have "the competence to carry out the job," and was "stunningly uninformed."[4] Trump's press secretary, Stephanie Grisham, was equally blunt: "[Trump] has no empathy, no morals, and no fidelity to the truth. He used to tell me, 'It doesn't matter what you say, Stephanie. Say it enough, and people will believe you.'"[5] Vice-President J.D. Vance used to go "back and forth between thinking Trump is a cynical asshole like Nixon . . . or that he's America's Hitler."[6]

How did Trump get to be such an empty, vengeful person? In no small part, he is the product of his mentorship with the notoriously ruthless, unprincipled lawyer, Roy Cohn. A young Donald Trump was infatuated with Cohn's aggressiveness and the way Cohn drew media attention to himself. He learned from Cohn what became Trump's approach to everything he does.[7] The first rule was always to attack, attack, attack. As Cohn put it, if someone comes at you with a knife, shoot back with a bazooka.

Cohn also taught Trump never to admit he was wrong. Deny everything. What you say becomes truth if you repeat it enough, Cohn believed. He taught Trump to portray himself as the victim, which Trump does regularly to deflect attention from his crimes. Trump also learned from Cohn that publicity was useful no matter what, and the more outrageous your statements, the more likely you would get coverage. Personal insults were an easy way to dominate news cycles. And lastly, Trump learned from Cohn how to use the law to harass opponents. Pursuing justice was irrelevant, and equally irrelevant was the truth of his allegations. His goal is to weaponize the legal system to get what he wants.[8]

Trump created his political base like other demagogues. He exploited people's personal frustrations and divided the world into "us" and "them." Anyone who opposed Trump was "nasty," "bad," and "evil." The more extreme the rhetoric the better. Democrats were "demonic," "Radical Leftists." Immigrants were "savages" and "vile animals" who would "walk in your kitchen and cut your throat." It was irrelevant that the crime rate among immigrants, including undocumented immigrants, was lower than for other people. What was important was inflaming his followers, making them as angry as possible, and using their anger to serve himself.

All of this formed an amoral witch's brew where the truth was irrelevant. Personal power and victory were all that mattered to Trump, and that meant winning re-election regardless of the actual vote. The Roy Cohn rules were ever-present in the election—first attack, then deny, and finally claim victory no matter what. That was Donald Trump.

Long before the first vote was cast, Trump set the stage for his narrative of stolen victory. If he lost, the election had to have been rigged. Trump had no intention of leaving the White House no matter what the outcome of the election. After the 2016 election, he claimed that he got 3 million fewer votes than Hilary Clinton only because millions of illegal votes had been cast, a claim that had no basis in fact. When asked if he would accept the results of the 2020 election, he refused to say he would—unless he won. To his millions of supporters, this wasn't just rhetoric—it was gospel. Chaos, violence, and "blood in the streets" were the price that Trump and his loyalists were willing to pay to resist a "steal."

Because of the Covid pandemic, mail-in voting was going to be especially important in 2020. Over and over, Trump incited his followers by saying that the election would be rigged and mail-in voting was fraudulent. He did that in anticipation of losing the mail-in vote in November. On May 24, 2020, he tweeted that mail-in ballots "will be the greatest Rigged Election in history. People grabbed them from mailboxes, print thousands of forgeries and 'force' people to sign. Also, forged names. Some absentee okay, when necessary."[9] To increase his followers' suspicions and anger, he told them mail-in ballots were controlled by foreign countries. On September 17, he tweeted: "There's a group of people (largely Radical Left Democrats) that want ELECTION MAYHEM. The states must end this CRAZY sending of ballots. Also, a GIFT to foreign interference in our election!!! Stop it now, before it is too late."[10] That the claim was completely made-up was not a problem; it had the desired effect. Even many non-MAGA Republicans fell into the Trump trap.

Trump knew the idea of foreign control was nonsense, so ridiculous he laughed when Sidney Powell told him over the speakerphone in the Oval

Office that she had just made those claims at a press conference. He muted the speaker while Powell was talking and said to others who were listening to the conversation, "This does sound crazy, doesn't it?"[11] No matter. Crazy as it was, it didn't stop him from continuing to say it.

Everyone knew before the 2020 election that Democratic and Republican votes don't come in uniformly during the day. Republicans voted more in person on election day, and Democratic voters tended to vote more frequently in advance of election day by mail-in and no-excuse absentee voting. Since some states count absentee and mail-in votes only after in-person votes are counted, Trump could be leading in early counts, but that lead would dissipate as all the votes were counted. Trump's campaign advisors knew this, of course, and so did Trump.

The 2020 election played out on November 3 as expected. Trump had an early lead, but it was expected to diminish. Bill Stepien, Trump's campaign manager, told Trump that his early public statement should say, "Votes are still being counted. It's too early to tell, too early to call the race, but we think we're in a good position."[12] Trump lied and announced the opposite that evening, claiming he had won and that any continued vote counting was fraudulent: "This is a fraud on the American people. This is an embarrassment to the country. We were getting ready to win this election. Frankly, we did win this election. We did win this election. . . . We want all voting to stop.[13] The next morning, Trump tweeted, "STOP THE COUNT!," his battle cry that would soon morph into "Stop the Steal."

Attorney General William Barr had been appointed by Trump and was very pro-Republican, so much so he had been criticized for pro-Trump bias in administering his office. But even he was taken aback at Trump's declaring victory and fraud since there was no evidence to support what Trump was saying. As Barr explained later:

> A lot of Democratic votes came in which changed the vote counts in certain states, and that would be the basis for [Trump's] claim that there was major

> fraud. And I didn't think much of that, because people had been talking for weeks and everyone understood for weeks that that was going to be what happened on election night.[14]

Trump's claim of fraud was no spur-of-the-moment outburst. He had been planning to falsely claim victory and fraud before the polls ever opened. On October 31, 2020, Trump's friend and advisor, Steve Bannon, told a group of his associates what Trump was going to do:

> What Trump's gonna do is just declare victory, right? He's gonna declare a victory. But that doesn't mean he's a winner. He's just gonna say he is a winner . . . The Democrats—more of our people voted early that count. There is mail-in vote. And so they're gonna have a natural disadvantage, and Trump's going to take advantage of it—that's our strategy. He's going to declare himself a winner. So when you wake up Wednesday morning, it's going to be a firestorm . . . Also, if Trump is losing by 10:00 or 11:00 at night, it's going to be even crazier. Because he is gonna sit right there and say, "They stole it." I'm directing the Attorney General to shut down all ballot places in all 50 states . . . [H]e's not going out easy. If Biden is winning, Trump is going to do some crazy shit.[15]

Trump confederate Roger Stone, best known for using the *National Enquirer* to "catch and kill" bad stories about Trump, said "I really do suspect [the election] will still be up in the air. When that happens, the key thing to do is to claim victory. Possession is nine-tenths of the law. No, we won. Fuck you, sorry. Over."[16]

Over the next few days, any slim chance Trump had to win disappeared as the vote count continued. On November 7, four days after the election, there was a meeting in the Oval Office where Trump was assured he would be the loser when every vote had been counted. Trump knew he had lost, but that didn't deter him from saying the opposite. While there was never any *evidence* of fraud that could conceivably have affected the outcome in any state, Trump grabbed every baseless, imaginary claim and shouted it to the world as if it were fact. Millions of his followers believed him, and that led to a further flood of crazy fraud allegations from people who *knew nothing* about the facts.

Over and over again, Trump was told by his own experts, campaign managers, and Attorney General that fraud had nothing to do with his losing the election. Telling Trump the truth about the election was a problem, though. He would disregard what he was told and sometimes fire the messenger. The Department of Justice and the FBI were sent on one wild-goose chase after another to track down every allegation. Barr told Trump on November 23 that the DOJ had investigated every fraud allegation that could conceivably have affected the election, but "they're just not meritorious. They're not panning out."[17] Barr wasn't alone. Other Justice Department officials *who Trump himself had appointed* repeatedly told him that the fraud allegations were false.

The truth didn't slow Trump down at all. His allegations just became more vehement and far-fetched. Trump jumped on the conspiracy theory that Dominion voting machines were "rigged" and changed votes from himself to Biden. He was told by his own campaign experts that was nonsense. The Department of Homeland Security was pulled into the fray and told him: "There is no evidence that any voting system deleted or lost votes, changed votes, or was in any way compromised."[18] Trump's response? Attack, deny, and claim victory. He tweeted and re-tweeted conspiracy theories about Dominion dozens of times *after he knew* they were just that—baseless conspiracy theories. Once again, the truth was irrelevant, but the tweets further enraged Trump's MAGA base, and the angrier they were, the better for Trump. They were being primed to help him keep the presidency regardless of the vote.

Bill Stepien and Justin Clark, the campaign's manager and deputy manager, respectively, drew the line at completely baseless conspiracy theories about election fraud. That meant they would soon be shunted aside. Trump wasn't going to have people that drew lines they wouldn't cross. The original campaign team was succeeded by a cabal best described as Team Crazy. Team Crazy's chief lawyer and most visible spokesperson was Rudy Giuliani. There were no lines he and Team Crazy wouldn't cross. The crazier the allegation the better. It was the Big Lie at its fullest.

Trump and Team Crazy were about to run into a problem, though. With all their allegations of illegal voting, Trump's supporters expected lawsuits where Trump would prove his claims and win. Republican legislators who were skeptical about the allegations had an easy response—file a lawsuit and with the evidence you have, you'll win. But that was a new thing for Trump. He was never about winning lawsuits. He was about bringing lawsuits to attack and harass people, not to prove his claims were true.

Trump and Republican Party allies filed sixty-two lawsuits in nine different states and the District of Columbia challenging the election. Not one found anything remotely like what Trump claimed. Repeatedly, judges condemned the plaintiffs for making wild accusations without any evidence to back them up. Typical of the rulings of dozens of federal and state judges are the following:

> **Arizona**: "The [plaintiffs'] 'expert reports' reach implausible conclusions, often because they are derived from wholly unreliable sources . . . Allegations that find favor in the public sphere of gossip and innuendo cannot be a substitute for earnest pleadings and procedure in federal court."[19]
>
> **Michigan**: The plaintiffs' case was "nothing but speculation and conjecture that votes for President Trump were destroyed, discarded or switched to votes for Vice President Biden."[20] The lawyers in that case were later sanctioned for their "historic and profound abuse of the judicial process" and trying to "deceive . . . the American people into believing that rights were infringed without regard to whether any laws or rights were in fact violated."[21]
>
> **Pennsylvania**: "Free, fair elections are the lifeblood of our democracy. Charges of unfairness are serious. But calling an election unfair does not

make it so. Charges require specific allegations and then proof. We have neither here."[22]

Nevada: "Contestants did not prove under any standard of proof that illegal votes were cast and counted, or legal votes were not counted at all, due to voter fraud, nor in an amount equal to or greater than 33,596 [the Biden vote advantage in Nevada], or otherwise in an amount sufficient to raise reasonable doubt as to the outcome of the election."[23]

Trump knew that courts were rejecting every claim he made in his "Stop the Steal" propaganda campaign. How did he react to losing all those cases? Roy Cohn lesson number two—deny and lie. Incredibly, Trump claimed that he *had proven* that the election was stolen but "no judge, including the Supreme Court of the United States, has had the courage to allow it to be heard."[24] In fact, some of his lawsuits were dismissed without a trial because the pleadings themselves were so ridiculous that they didn't even state a legal claim, which is the lowest bar for a plaintiff to get over. Some others were voluntarily dismissed by the plaintiffs' lawyers, likely because they feared being sanctioned for bringing frivolous cases. But thirty of Trump's sixty-two cases were dismissed after a full hearing on the merits. Twenty-two of the federal judges who oversaw the cases were appointed by Republican presidents, ten by Trump himself.

Undeterred, Trump used *losing* his lawsuits to further whip up his base by accusing the courts of being corrupt! That fed right into the MAGA mindset and further angered his minions; they were ready to do his bidding. Trump personally called state officials to try to get them to falsify the election returns, and he turned his MAGA dogs loose on them to maximize the pressure. The most infamous of Trump's calls was to Georgia Secretary of State Brad Raffensperger. Expecting the worst, Raffensperger had refused to return Trump's calls for weeks, but he finally spoke with him and recorded the call, unbeknownst to Trump. In that call, Trump cajoled, pressured, and threatened Raffensberger to *find* enough votes to change the outcome. "All I want to do is this. I just want to find 11,780 votes . . ."[25]

The call went on at length and Trump and his Chief of Staff, Mark Meadows, reiterated one debunked claim after another. Trump falsely said "4,502 who voted [in Georgia] weren't on the voter registration roll, which they had to be, . . . and there were 18,325 vacant address voters." Raffensperger replied, "Well, Mr. President . . . the data you have is wrong." Trump next tried his made-up claim about dead voters: "Dead people voted, and I think the number is close to 5,000 people. And they went to obituaries. They went to all sorts of methods to come up with an accurate number, and a minimum is close to about 5,000 voters." Raffensperger replied, "The actual number were two. Two people that were dead that voted." Increasingly frustrated by Raffensperger's unwillingness to help him steal the election, Trump moved to thinly veiled threats that Raffensperger was committing a crime by *not* changing the vote!

> It is more illegal for you than it is for them because, you know what they did and you're not reporting it. That's a criminal, that's a criminal offense. And you can't let that happen. That's a big risk to you and to Ryan, your lawyer. And that's a big risk . . . Under the law you're not allowed to give faulty election results, OK? You're not allowed to do that. And that's what you've done. This is a faulty election result.[26]

Trump told Raffensperger he would be punished by Trump's cadres if he didn't do what he was told, and Trump made good on his threats. He continued to repeat his false claims about Georgia's vote, putting election officials in danger of their lives. Even before the phone call, Trump's drumbeat of false tweets about Raffensperger had caused death threats. Raffensperger's Chief Operating Officer, Gabriel Sterling, held a press conference where he made a passionate, angry plea to Trump and Republican leaders to stop inciting the election deniers:

> [I]t has all gone too far. . . . A 20-something [election] tech in Gwinnett County today has death threats and a noose put out, saying he should be

> hung for treason because he was transferring a report on batches from an EMS to a county computer so he could read it. It has to stop. *Mr. President, you have not condemned these actions or this language.* Senators, you have not condemned this language or these actions. This has to stop . . . This is elections, this is the backbone of democracy, and all of you who have not said a damn word are complicit in this . . . Stop inspiring people to commit potential acts of violence. Someone's going to get hurt. Someone's going to get shot. Someone's going to get killed.[27]

Sterling's words fell on deaf ears. Trump continued to inflame his followers with a steady stream of lies. The result? Arizona Secretary of State Katie Hobbs received hundreds of threats, a voicemail that said, "You'll never be safe in Arizona again," and the following social media post: "Let's burn her house down and kill her family and teach these fraudsters a lesson."[28] The same threats and worse occurred in all the battleground states. In Georgia, the Fulton County Elections Director, Richard Barron, was singled out by Trump in a video at a rally prompting death threats to him and his staff. One man telephoned Ralph Jones, Barron's registration chief, and called him a "nigger who should be shot." Another threatened to kill him "by dragging his body around with a truck."[29]

In typical Trump fashion, his tweets about the election served a secondary purpose—money. Between the election and January 6, 2021, he raised *$250 million dollars* in response to his false claims that the election was rigged and fraudulent. His pleas to "loyal" Republicans assured them their donations could stop Democrats from "trying to steal the election" and prevent Biden from taking office as an "illegitimate president."[30]

Because the Constitution gives state legislatures the power to determine how a state's electoral votes are determined, Team Crazy came up with an idea to circumvent the 2020 election completely—have the legislatures in the swing states that Biden won assign their electors to Trump *regardless of the vote.* On

November 25, Republican legislators from Pennsylvania met in a hotel ballroom and heard wild claims of fraud from Giuliani and other members of Team Crazy, all the same litany of nonsense that had been thoroughly debunked already. The leader of the pack was State Senator Doug Mastriano, a prime mover in the Stop the Steal insurrection. Trump phoned into the meeting and was cheered as he ticked off his litany of election fraud claims, all of which he knew to be false. He told the gathered legislators, "This election has to be turned around." Another member of Team Crazy told them it was in their power as legislators to designate Pennsylvania's electors. "You can take that power at any time. You don't need a court to tell you that."[31]

Similar meetings occurred in Arizona, Michigan, and Georgia. Always, there were some Republican legislators who were only too eager to curry favor with Trump and keep a right-wing president in the White House, despite who voters had chosen. Legislators and governors who opposed Trump's call to appoint substitute electors were condemned and threatened.

Still, Trump and his confederates couldn't convince enough Republican governors and legislators to so blatantly violate their own state law, so they shifted to a backup plan that could allow him to hang on to the White House. They would create fake electors without the blessing of the state legislatures. Under the Constitution, the Vice President, Michael Pence, was charged with opening the electors' certificates. The idea of having a separate set of electors had been germinating since the election, and with Trump's other options for stealing the presidency fading, the fake elector scheme took on a new urgency.

The plan again focused on the battleground states Biden had won, plus New Mexico, and it was carried out by Team Crazy with help from Republican National Committee Chairwoman, Ronna McDaniel, some members of Congress, and Republican Party officials in those states. In the hope of adding some colorable legitimacy to their flagrantly illegal scheme, the initial plan was to have the alternative electors be the same people who had been designated as Trump electors and would have served in that capacity had he won those states' elections. Many of them agreed to join the scam without a second thought. Some others who had doubts agreed to join the conspiracy anyhow.

The lawyers with Trump's campaign team had supported the election litigation, frivolous as it was, but they were squeamish about the fake elector plan. As long as there was some case pending that challenged the election, no matter how far-fetched it might be, they rationalized that the fake electors could be justified as a "contingent" slate—they would become electors only if a court reversed the election in their state. But with no remaining case that could change any state's election outcome, the fake elector scheme was too much for the original campaign lawyers. No problem. Trump's Team Crazy took over.

Fake elector certificates were ginned up in each state. Some of the fake electors who had doubts about the legality of what they were doing were assured that the certificates would only be used if a court changed the outcome of their state's election. As January 6, 2021, approached, however, there were no cases pending that remotely held any such promise. Trump's team still tried to use the fake certificates.

Trump's fraudulent elector scheme reminded historians of the Tilden-Hayes election a century and a half earlier. Republicans justified what they were doing with the same ploy their predecessors had done in 1877 by claiming that Pence could be the "ultimate arbiter" of the electoral votes and decide which set of electors would be counted. They forgot that the last time that argument was tried it nearly pushed the country into a second civil war.

On November 29, Trump appeared on *Fox News* and spewed his debunked conspiracy theories—the election was rigged, Dominion machines changed votes, there had been "vote dumps," dead voters, and on and on. He rambled on incoherently: "this is total fraud, and how the FBI and Department of Justice—I don't know, maybe they are involved—and how people are getting away with this stuff—is unbelievable."[32]

Attorney General Barr finally had too much. Trump had not only complained that the DOJ was not doing anything, which was false, but now insinuated that the agency might even be "in on the fraud." Barr met with a journalist and told him the truth, that the DOJ and FBI had investigated *every one* of Trump's claims and they were all baseless. The next day's headline reporting Barr's comments got him an immediate summons to the White House. Trump was so furious he wouldn't even look at Barr, and his fleshy face was red with anger. Fuming, Trump shoved a newspaper at Barr and erupted, "This is, you know, killing me. You didn't have to say this. You must have said this because you hate Trump—You hate Trump." It was very strange how Trump spoke of himself in the third person, but Barr had seen that before. He replied that he didn't "hate Trump" and reminded him that he had agreed to join the administration to help Trump when he was at a low point. Barr explained again that the actual *evidence* refuted every one of the conspiracy theories. Trump's reaction to hearing the *facts* again? He made a Facebook video regurgitating all the claims he knew were false. Barr resigned, effective December 14. He explained later:

> I did not agree with the idea of saying the election was stolen and putting out this stuff, which I told the president was bullshit. I didn't want to be part of it . . . I believe you can't live in a world where the incumbent administration stays in power based on its view, unsupported by evidence, that the election—that there was fraud in the election.[33]

With Barr gone, Jeffrey Rosen became Acting Attorney General and Richard Donoghue his deputy, both steadfast Republicans. To Trump, the DOJ was just another arm of his personal election campaign that should do his bidding. He was angry when he saw that Rosen and Donoghue were like Barr when it came to the election. They were standing by the DOJ–FBI investigations that found *nothing* to support any claim that Biden had won the election by fraudulent means.

That made Trump and Team Crazy redouble their efforts to corrupt the Justice Department, since their other options to steal the election weren't panning out. State election officials were refusing to falsify the election results, state legislatures were refusing to circumvent the elections and appoint fake electors, and Trump and his Republican allies were losing in court. If they could just get the DOJ to endorse their fraud claims, they thought that could change the public dynamic. Relatively few members of the public in 2021 would have thought that the DOJ would completely fabricate claims of election fraud unless there was something to them. That was before Pam Bondi and Kash Patel would make dishonesty a prime feature of the DOJ's identity. In 2021, Trump had to get past Acting Attorney General Rosen to get the DOJ to peddle his fake claims.

A way around Rosen's resistance was suggested by Pennsylvania Congressman Scott Perry, a prime mover in the Stop the Steal campaign. He proposed to Team Crazy and Trump that Jeffrey Clark—an assistant attorney general with no experience in elections, criminal investigations, or fraud cases—would be the right man for the job, a man willing to say anything for Trump. On December 27, Trump called Rosen and Donoghue and told them that Perry and Ohio Congressman Jim Jordan—a loud-mouthed right-winger who avoided the truth whenever it got in his way—had told Trump that his allegations were true. In fact, neither of them had any actual knowledge about Trump's claims; they were simply two election deniers who parroted the usual conspiracy theories without any *evidence* to back them up.

When Rosen and Donoghue again explained to Trump that there was no evidence to support his claims, Trump's response was shockingly absurd: "You guys must not be following the internet the way I do."[34] Rosen reiterated that the Department couldn't file a case without real facts. But Trump couldn't care less whether there was any merit to a DOJ lawsuit so long as it *alleged* voting irregularities. He told them to file a case regardless. "*Just say the election is corrupt and leave the rest to me and the Republican congressmen.*"[35] Donoghue was so stunned by Trump's unabashed willingness to corrupt the Department of Justice and the election that that "exact quote from the President" was etched in his memory.

With Barr having just resigned as Attorney General, it would be better for public appearances if Trump could circumvent Rosen rather than fire him outright. Team Crazy assigned Assistant Attorney General Clark the task of drafting a letter to the battleground states that would endorse Trump's false claims of election fraud. When Rosen and Donoghue saw the draft letter, which would be issued under their signatures, they were irate. It said that the DOJ had "identified significant concerns that may have impacted the outcome of the election" and that the state in question should call a special session to take additional testimony and receive new evidence about the election. The draft letter also treated the fake electors as a legitimate "competing" set of electors for Congress to consider, rather than part of an illegal coup attempt.

Trump hoped that the Justice Department imprimatur on his claims would bolster his chance of stealing the election, but Donaghue was livid when he saw the draft letter and emailed Clark immediately: "There is no chance that I would sign this letter, or anything remotely like this." If anything like it were sent, Donoghue went on, "it would be a grave step for the Department to take and it could have tremendous Constitutional, political and social ramifications for the country."[36] Rosen was equally adamant when the three of them had a fractious meeting in the Justice Department, an historic Depression era building where hundreds of other meetings had carved out the country's legal history.

The next day, December 29, Rosen and Donoghue were told that the president wanted the DOJ to file a lawsuit against Pennsylvania, and they were given a draft of a complaint Team Crazy had prepared. The complaint made no sense, and there was no evidence to back it up. It was just one more trip down conspiracy lane, and both men refused to file it.

On December 30, Trump telephoned Rosen in another effort to get him to file *United States vs. Pennsylvania.* Rosen refused, but Trump and his allies wouldn't back off. The next day was New Year's Eve, and Trump summoned Rosen and Donoghue to the White House and raised the idea of making Jeffrey

Clark the Acting Attorney General. He also raised the possibility of naming a special counsel to investigate the "election crimes," but Rosen and Donoghue said that couldn't be done because there was "no evidence" that there had been any crimes. Trump didn't care; he wanted something done to give credence to his litany of falsehoods.

Frustrated that the DOJ wouldn't file a bogus election case, Trump threw out a new idea he thought might create enough confusion he could exploit to disrupt Biden's election victory. "Why don't you guys seize the voting machines? You guys should seize the machines because they'll be evidence."[37] Rosen explained that nothing could be seized without a search warrant and reiterated that there was no evidence to justify a warrant.

Blocked by Rosen, Trump secretly asked Clark to be the Acting Attorney General. On Saturday, January 2, Rosen and Donoghue again met with Clark, and Clark acknowledged that Trump had offered him Rosen's job. He told Rosen and Donoghue that he would decline the offer *if* they agreed to sign his scam letter to the states. Presumably, Trump had worked out that strategy with Clark in the hope of getting the letters Trump wanted sent without having to fire Rosen, but both Rosen and Donoghue again refused to sign.

The next day, Clark spoke with Trump several times and they agreed he would take over as Acting Attorney General, but as word of their plot reverberated through the Justice Department, there was an upsurge of anger and disgust at what Trump was doing. One of the senior DOJ attorneys, Patrick Hovakimian, drafted a letter of resignation that explained he was leaving because Rosen was being fired for "refusing the President's direct instructions to utilize the Department of Justice's law enforcement powers for improper ends."[38] That was strong language for a DOJ lawyer to put in a letter to a president, and when it became public, which it inevitably would, Trump would suffer a firestorm of negative publicity.

Before Clark's appointment was announced, Rosen, Donoghue, and Trump met in the Oval Office on the evening of January 3. Also at the meeting were

Clark, Chief of Staff Mark Meadows, and White House counsel Pat Cipollone. Rosen and Donoghue stood fast and told Trump they would resign if Clark was made Acting Attorney General. Donoghue went on to tell Trump that the entire leadership of the DOJ, who had been appointed by Trump himself, would resign. "What is that going to say about you, when we all walk out at the same time," he asked Trump, "and what happens if within 48 hours, we have hundreds of resignations from your trusted Department because of your actions?"[39]

Trump knew they were right. The public uproar would be deafening. It would be the whole DOJ, in effect, quitting rather than capitulating to Trump's illegal demands. Trump was boxed in and angrily agreed not to appoint Clark. For the moment, a constitutional crisis had been averted at the eleventh hour, a crisis caused by Trump's willingness to do anything to hold onto the White House. But Trump wasn't finished.

Trump had his army of followers he had convinced that the election was being stolen. The most extreme brigades in his army were right-wing militias like the Oath Keepers and Proud Boys who were violently anti-government. As the Proud Boys' founder said, "We will kill you. That's the Proud Boys in a nutshell."[40] Trump had used his angry army to harass and intimidate election officials and state legislatures. He was ready now to call on them again, this time to hijack the counting of electoral votes at the Capitol.

January 6, 2021, was the date when Vice President Michael Pence would open the envelopes containing each state's electoral votes. The votes would be presented to Congress, unless there were objections to a given state's certificate. The idea that Pence alone had the authority to determine the validity of a state's votes had been bandied about for weeks, but it had taken on a new importance as other avenues to steal the election eluded Trump. John Eastman, an ultra-conservative law professor at Claremont College, became the principal advocate that Pence had unlimited power. As a backup strategy, Eastman argued that Pence could at least claim there were contested votes, delay the count, and send everything back to the states to reconsider. At times, Eastman acknowledged that his plans were illegal and not one member of the Supreme Court would buy what he was selling.

Trump used his online militia to harass and threaten Pence and Congress, but he wasn't going to stop there. He was ready for a violent insurrection if that's what it took to hold on to the presidency. He tweeted his followers on December 19, "Big protest in D.C. on January 6. Be there, will be wild!"[41] The same day, Trump tweeted a video titled "FIGHT FOR TRUMP!—SAVE AMERICA—SAVE THE WORLD"[42] that would become a rallying cry for Trump's mob.

Trump had lit the fuse, and the militias heard Trump's call to arms. Minutes after Trump's tweet, one post on a right-wing message board said, "Trump Tweet. Daddy Says Be in DC on Jan. 6th."[43] The Proud Boys were big Trump admirers, and he treated them more like a legitimate group than the violent thugs they admitted to being. They were enthusiastic about being called to Washington. The Oath Keepers stored military grade weapons near Washington in the hope Trump would deputize them.[44] Right-wing talk show hosts like Alex Jones, an expert at making up baseless conspiracies to generate listeners and line his pockets, added fuel to what could become an inferno. He told people to go to Washington for Trump. "He's calling *you*, he needs your help, we need your help."[45] Most of the anti-government militia members believed Trump when he said the election had been stolen, but some didn't care. They just wanted a right-wing president no matter how he got to the White House. Trump was their man.

Trump's call to come to Washington and "be wild" unleashed a torrent of invective on the internet and social media to overthrow the U.S. government. As January 6 approached, the Secret Service and FBI saw more and more ominous signs that the day could be violent. Pence never had the backbone to come out and say what the Department of Justice and FBI had told him, that the claims of fraud and voting irregularities were baseless. Instead, on

January 2, he issued a statement saying that he shared "the concerns of millions of Americans about voter fraud" and "welcomes the efforts of members of Congress . . . to raise objections and bring forward evidence before the Congress and the American people on January 6."[46] Pence was trying to have it both ways. He told everyone around him that Eastman's ideas were crazy and illegal, but the sympathy he expressed for the election deniers emboldened them. Had he spoken the truth on January 2, his words would have lowered the temperature.

Trump knew the Eastman plan was illegal—Eastman had said as much in Trump's presence. Regardless, if he could get Pence to go along with Eastman's plans, Trump thought he could stay in the White House. He falsely tweeted that Pence had the "power to reject fraudulently chosen electors," and he even said that Pence *agreed* he had the power to change the election.[47] That was just another Trump lie to add to the thousands that were piling up. Pence never said or insinuated anything like that to Trump or anyone else.

Trump called Pence to the Oval Office on January 5 and had the kind of bizarre conversation that only Trump can have. In discussing whether Pence could unilaterally determine the electoral votes, Trump asked: "Wouldn't it almost be cool to have that power?" Pence replied, "I've done everything I could and then some to find a way around this. It's simply not possible." Infuriated, Trump shouted, "No, no, no! You don't understand, Mike. You can do this. *I don't want to be your friend anymore if you don't do this.*"[48] Trump so often acted like a churlish brat, no one was surprised by what he said to Pence.

Over 50,000 people came to Washington to "go wild" for Trump, and he continued to inflame them to the last minute. On the evening of January 5, the crowd listened to incendiary speeches from conspiracists and election deniers while Trump tweeted: "All of us here today do not want to see our election victory stolen by emboldened Radical Left Democrats. Our Country has had enough, they won't take it anymore! Together, we will STOP THE STEAL."[49]

On the morning of the 6th, Trump's speechwriters tried to steer him away from his most vicious attacks, but that wasn't Trump's way. When he spoke to the crowd in the Ellipse, he adlibbed for nearly an hour, railing against Pence and demanding that Republicans in Congress send the electoral votes back to the states.

Trump's "back to the states" ploy sounded like a delaying tactic in the hope that Republicans could finally get the legislatures in those states to designate electors for him, but it was much more insidious than that. Under the Constitution, if no one receives a majority of the electoral votes for president, the House of Representatives chooses the president, but not all representatives are created equal in that vote. Instead, those from rural Republican states have far more power because *each state gets one vote*, and that would have given Republicans a twenty-six to twenty-three majority (Pennsylvania's delegation was split evenly). If Trump could just get some of the battleground states to withdraw their original electors under the guise of "confusion" he might still have a path to steal the election. He didn't need those states to send an alternate set of delegates—no delegates at all would work just as well.

Trump reveled in the seething anger of the crowd. "We will not let them silence your voices," Trump screamed. "We're not gonna let it happen, I'm not, I'm not gonna let it happen." People yelled back, "Fight for Trump!" and he told them, "We fight like hell. And if you don't fight like hell, you're not going to have a country anymore."

Trump knew how dangerous the mob was when half of the 50,000 people who were at the Ellipse to hear him refused to go through metal detectors because they didn't want their guns confiscated by the Secret Service. Trump was furious and demanded that they be allowed to pass without going through the detectors. "I don't fucking care that they have weapons. They're not here to hurt *me*,"[50] Trump yelled. Violent, armed militiamen were exactly what Trump needed for his last-ditch effort to steal the election. Words and threats hadn't gotten him what he wanted yet. If he was going to change the electoral vote count, he needed more drastic action.

When Trump finished his speech, the crowd had already begun its attack on the Capitol. Pence began the opening and recording of electoral votes at 1:00 p.m. and was calling for any objections when it became clear that Republicans were going to object to all the states Trump wanted challenged. The first one was Arizona, and it was being debated in the Senate Chamber when the proceedings were stopped by the mob that had marched from the Ellipse. The next several hours witnessed unbridled mayhem, as the rioters rampaged through the Capitol looking for Pence, among others, while chanting "Hang Mike Pence." Trump watched what was happening on TV at the White House and was bombarded by people asking him to condemn the riot and tell the rioters to stop and leave, but he refused. It was *his* riot, and the rioters were doing what he wanted.

An hour and a half into the riot, Trump made his first statement, and it was one of the most appalling addresses any American president ever made. He used his election lies to *justify* the riot and blame Pence!

> Mike Pence didn't have the courage to do what should have been done to protect our Country and our Constitution, giving States a chance to certify a corrected set of facts, not the fraudulent or inaccurate ones which they were asked to previously certify. USA demands the truth![51]

After three hours of rioting and destruction at the Capitol, as well as injuries and death, Trump finally agreed to call it off. But again, instead of condemning or criticizing the rioters in any way, he ignored the prepared text and continued to praise them while repeating the Big Lie about the election:

> I know your pain. I know you're hurt. We had an election that was stolen from us. It was a landslide election, and everyone knows it . . . So go home, we love you. You're very special . . . You see the way others are treated that

> are so bad and so evil. I know how you feel but go home and go home in peace.[52]

What happened next was extraordinary. People in the mob were watching his statement on their phones, and as soon as he was done, word spread that Trump had told them to go home. They immediately packed up and left. If there had been the slightest question before that moment whether the crowd was completely under Trump's control, there was no question any longer. It was his mob, his riot.

When Congress convened later that day to continue the electoral vote count, a majority voted to accept Arizona's electors, but 121 Republican congressman and six Republican senators voted to reject them. They had joined Trump's effort to steal the presidency. After Arizona, the electoral votes of the other states were accepted without objection since it was clear how the vote would go.

Another constitutional crisis had been narrowly avoided, but one could only wonder how many more Republican congressmen would have voted to reject Arizona's electors if Trump had not terrified them by summoning his militia to attack the Capitol. The 2000 presidential election left a scar on the idea that the United States was a democracy governed by law, but that steal—even though it succeeded—was nothing compared to what Trump did to the country in 2020. The division between our people is now wider and sharper than ever. Facts are no longer facts; they are whatever you say they are. Years later, with every one of Trump's stolen election claims completely debunked, an astonishing 63 percent of Republicans still believe the lie that the election was stolen *from* Trump.

Leaders of democratic countries were dumbfounded at the election and the attack on the Capitol. Putin, Xi Jinping, Kim Jong Un, and other autocrats were overjoyed. Trump had done more to shatter the reputation and authority of the United States than all of their efforts combined.

9

Voter Suppression in the 21st Century

Stealing elections is as much a national blight today as ever, but it's not done by stuffing ballot boxes. What Talmadge did in 1947, what Texas Senate candidates did in the 1940s, and what Hurst did to Carter in 1962 is not really possible with modern technology. But old-school voter suppression to whittle down opposition voters is thriving today and drawing on the lessons of the past. Republicans, threatened by minorities and young people who vote Democratic, have been passing a raft of new laws to make voting more difficult.

Republicans don't need a white primary to eliminate African American voters. They learned in the 2000 election that they can steal the presidency itself with a voter purge like the one that year in Florida. They saw again in 2020 how a few votes in the right place can change who is president. In 2020, Arizona went for Biden by 0.3 percent and Georgia by 0.2 percent. The "value" to Republicans of tightening voting access to eliminate Democratic voters was obvious. As Sara Ghazal, a member of the Georgia State Board of Elections put it, "They only have to make voting marginally more difficult for voters on the margin since the slightest nudge will push them over the edge."

Since the South has an especially sordid history of voter suppression, it isn't surprising that the South "rose again" when Republicans took over Southern legislatures in the 1990s and 2000s. The new Republicans of the South were not at all like the Southern Republicans from earlier decades who were often Republican because they couldn't abide Southern Democrats' stand on segregation. The new Southern Republicans were just the opposite. They were the worst of the racist and right-wing Democrats who left that party when it did an about face on civil rights under Lyndon Johnson. They were offered a new home in the Republican Party where there would be no more talk of civil rights. To these new Southern Republicans, voter suppression was a natural. It was what their ancestors had practiced for generations, and George Wallace's racist cry that voting need to be restricted to avoid "fraud" still echoed in their memories.

Justifying restrictive voting laws took some fancy footwork. Voter suppression enthusiasts needed to convince people that voting needed to be harder to do. If there was widespread voter fraud, Republican legislators could slide through vote suppression laws in the name of "stopping the fraud." There was only one problem with the Republican strategy—*the truth*. Claims of vote fraud were complete fiction.

Dozens if not hundreds of rigorous studies of vote fraud claims have all come to the same conclusion.[1] Voter fraud is extremely rare, and what might initially be claimed as some indication of fraud is almost always something else when looked at closely. Ironically, a result of the proliferation of new voting restrictions is that "[t]he more complex are the rules regulating voter registration and voting, the more likely voter mistakes, clerical errors, and the like will be wrongly identified as 'fraud.'"[2] One exhaustive study in 2014 searched for cases of voter impersonation and identified thirty-one *possible* instances *out of a billion votes cast*.[3] Other elections that have been studied for fraud have found rates between 0.0003 percent and 0.0025 percent,[4] rates so slight they fall well below the level of random, innocent tabulation errors.

But facts weren't enough to stop voter suppression laws. They were just an inconvenience. The facts could be changed with a flood of propaganda to fit the Republican narrative. All they needed to do was yell "voter fraud" loud enough and often enough and people would believe there was fraud. Advertisers, politicians, and psychologists know that people are more likely to believe what they hear often, even if it's a lie.[5] Angry cries of fraud stick in our minds while deliberate, detailed studies that refute those claims are barely heard and quickly forgotten.

Twenty years ago, a Republican Senate Policy Committee report made the frightening statement that "voter fraud continues to plague our nation's federal elections, diluting and *canceling out the lawful votes of the vast majority of Americans*."[6] The statement was absolute nonsense, and Republicans knew it was nonsense. But their report wasn't designed to educate anyone about the facts. Its sole purpose was to rile up voters to support new voting restrictions. As one election expert said about the report: "The claim that voter fraud threatens the integrity of American elections is itself a fraud. It is being used to persuade the public that deceitful and criminal voters are manipulating the electoral system."[7]

Vote suppression advocates often refer to "evidence" of fraud that actually says the opposite—or in many cases doesn't exist at all. Donald Trump is the King of Election Lies and has spread every imaginable false voting claim, most notoriously, of course, that the 2020 election was "stolen" from him. Were it not for Trump's massive shadow, Kris Koback might be the country's greatest purveyor of false election claims. He certainly worked hard for the crown when he was the Kansas Secretary of State. Kobach implemented exceptionally strict voter identification laws that would remove 20,000 legitimate voters from the state's rolls, his efforts justified by a flood of bogus claims of "widespread election fraud."

Kobach embraced Trump's idiotic claim that "millions" of people voted illegally for Hillary Clinton in 2016, but not a scintilla of evidence substantiated their made-up claim.[8] In another outburst of propaganda, Kobach called a press conference to complain that 2,000 people supposedly voted in Kansas under the names of dead people. When the local press investigated the one example of a possible "dead voter" he named, it turned out that the man was very much alive.[9]

After years spreading false rumors of voter fraud, it came time for Republicans to reap the fruits of their lies. In the Southern states, new voter suppression laws were generally blocked by Section 5 of the Voting Rights Act, but Republican-controlled legislatures elsewhere saw their opportunity and ran with it. They homed in on new voter identification requirements as a perfect way to suppress minority and Democratic voters in the name of "fraud prevention." Their propaganda had been so pervasive that the electorate and the courts were ready to swallow what looked like a common-sense law to stop the plague of voter fraud. That the real purpose of the new laws was to give Republicans an edge in elections was kept close to the vest.

Indiana was one of the first states to pass a voter photo ID law in 2005. Though Indiana had *no* history of people showing up to vote and claiming they were someone else, voters would now have to produce a photo ID from a government agency before they could cast a ballot in person. There had been some history of questionable absentee voting in the state, but Indiana's new law did nothing to address that issue. Why not? Because absentee voting was used more by Republican voters, so a little fraud could be tolerated to keep those votes coming. Every single Republican legislator voted for Indiana's ID law, and every single Democratic legislator voted against it, a pretty good indication of who it would help and who it would hurt.

When Indiana's law got to the Supreme Court, Justice Stevens wrote the opinion for himself, Roberts, and Kennedy upholding the law, and Stevens had obviously been seduced by the Republican propaganda machine. He wrote that the law was justified by the state's interest in preventing "in-person voter impersonation at polling places" even though there was "no evidence of any such fraud occurring in Indiana *at any time in its history*"![10] Stevens thought stopping "fraud" was so important the law was justified nonetheless.

Stevens also rationalized the ID requirement as a way to bolster "public confidence in the integrity of the electoral process." Once again, he had swallowed the Republican Red Pill of illusion. "Public confidence" in elections had taken a hit only *because of Republican propaganda proclaiming voter fraud*. Moreover, the states with the most restrictive voter ID laws have the highest levels of public distrust in their elections, not *increased* public confidence! If Indiana really wanted to enhance voter confidence, it wouldn't have thrown more fuel on the myth of fraud by passing a voter ID law. Instead, it would have told the public the truth, admitted there was no voter impersonation in Indiana, and renounced the Fraud Lie.

Justice Souter dissented after pointing out the obvious—that many thousands of Indiana "voting-age residents lack the necessary photo identification, [and] a large proportion of them are likely to be in bad shape economically." The burden on those people to get a photo ID was real, both economically and because of their limited mobility and limited capacity to navigate what to most people is just a bureaucratic hurdle, but to others is an insurmountable barrier.

Stevens later realized that all the noise about voter fraud was just that, noise. He admitted after he retired that "David Souter got the thing correct" and "as a matter of actual history, he's dead right. The impact of the [Indiana ID] statute is much more serious" on poor, minority, disabled, and elderly voters than he had realized.[11] The author of the Seventh Circuit opinion that upheld the Indiana law, Richard Posner, did the same thing. Posner is a very conservative judge who later said he was "absolutely wrong" in upholding the law and blamed his error on the lack of evidence in the trial record to prove it would "actually disenfranchise people entitled to vote."[12] That excuse is awfully flimsy, especially since another judge on the same panel realized what the law would do. As Judge Evans wrote in his dissent, "Let's not beat around the bush: The Indiana voter photo ID law is a not-too-thinly-veiled attempt to discourage election-day turnout by certain folks believed to skew Democratic."[13]

To anyone that has ever worked on the ground in voter turnout, the impact of voter ID laws is obvious. They do exactly what Judge Evans said they would and what the Indiana legislature intended—reduce Democratic vote shares by keeping minority and poor people from voting. In one study that examined the impact of the Texas ID law in a specific congressional race, it found that the outcome of the election was flipped by the ID requirement. The Democratic candidate, Pete Gallego, lost to his Republican rival, Will Hurd, because of vote suppression caused by the ID requirement. Gallego would have won without the ID requirement.[14] Other studies have shown that the impact is very real and that minorities are affected substantially more than whites.[15] That is hardly surprising given the wealth gap between whites and non-whites.

Vote fraud propaganda has worked wonders for Republican efforts to pass voter ID laws. In 2000, thirty-six states had no specific ID requirement, and only four required a photo ID. Even in those four states, the overall requirements were considered "non-strict" by the National Conference of State Legislatures.[16] By 2016, eight states had adopted strict ID requirements with a photo; only seventeen had no ID requirement. Today, only fourteen states do not require documentation to vote at the polls, and ten have both a strict ID and photo requirement.[17]

Even Congress has partly succumbed to the propaganda about voter ID. Largely in response to the Florida punch card disaster in the 2000 presidential election, Congress passed the Help America Voter Act (HAVA) in 2002 to replace punch card and "lever-pull" voting machines. To pass the bill, Republicans insisted that it include a requirement that first-time voters who register by mail must present some form of identification when they vote. That can be a current photo ID *or* a utility bill *or* another document with the name and address of the voter. While the HAVA requirement is mild compared to many state ID requirements, it gave legitimacy to photo IDs. In the Indiana case, Justice Stevens bolstered his opinion by noting that "Congress believes that photo identification is one effective method of establishing a voter's qualification to vote."

The Supreme Court's decision in the Indiana ID case was bad enough, but the court wasn't close to finished with its crusade to roll back federal voting protections. It had already carved off a big piece of Section 2 when it put many discriminatory election practices outside the statute's reach by disregarding the language of the statute and the congressional report that explained how claims of voting discrimination should be decided.[18] "Strict construction" and "textualism"—which the conservative justices throw around when convenient to deny civil rights claims—are nowhere to be seen when those rules get in the way of the result they want to reach.

The Supreme Court outdid itself in 2013 when it erased Section 5 in the *Shelby County* case.[19] Chief Justice Roberts wrote that ultra-radical opinion, and he was devious. The court didn't explicitly strike down Section 5, but instead ruled that the "coverage formula" that determined which states and counties were subject to Section 5 was "unconstitutionally out of date." Theoretically, *Shelby* left open the possibility that the coverage formula could be revised by Congress and Section 5 could once again take effect. But Roberts knew that Congress wouldn't agree on a different formula, and even if it did, there was no formula the Supreme Court would ever agree was constitutional. Section 5 was dead. The formula rationale Roberts trotted out was just a ruse to mask how extreme the decision was and to deflect criticism from the court to Congress.

Shelby was not just extreme in its result. It was an unprecedented appropriation of congressional authority. Congress had a vast record before it in 2006 that established the need to extend Section 5 under the existing coverage formula, but Roberts didn't care. In his *personal opinion*, Section 5 was "unnecessary." One can agree or disagree with the necessity of Section 5, but that wasn't for Roberts or the Supreme Court to decide. That decision was vested by the Constitution in Congress. Laws can be declared unconstitutional if they violate a provision of the Constitution, but there isn't a single word in the Constitution that was contradicted by Section 5 of the Voting Rights Act.

As much as anything, *Shelby* stands for John Roberts' revenge. When he was at the Justice Department as a twenty-six-year-old lawyer, Roberts was rabid in his opposition to amending the Voting Rights Act to replace *Mobile*'s intent test with a results test—the same results test I testified in favor of before the House and Senate subcommittees in 1981 and 1982.[20] Roberts drafted memoranda opposing the Section 2 amendment, prepared administration officials for their testimony before the Senate, and lobbied the most conservative senators and their staff in the hope of killing the bill.

At the same time, Roberts tried to convince the Justice Department to intervene in the Burke County case I was about to argue in the Supreme Court in February 1982, and to intervene *on the side of Burke County in defense of its white supremacist political system!* Roberts drafted a brief for the Solicitor General to file, but lawyers in the Civil Rights Division drafted a counter brief that showed how extreme Roberts' views were. In the end, he was thwarted, but just barely. So, at one time I stood two wins and no losses in my encounters with Roberts. Now, forty years later, Roberts has fulfilled his *personal* mission to destroy the Voting Rights Act.

Shelby generated absolute jubilation from white Republicans in the South and deep anxiety among African Americans. North Carolina Republicans wanted to reverse years of African American voting gains immediately, but they were so excited they forgot to temper their new laws with "plausible deniability." The legislature had been planning to pass a relatively narrow ID bill, but the day *Shelby* was decided Republicans began adding new restrictions to the bill like ornaments on a *Shelby* Christmas tree. They feasted like the men at the 1890 Mississippi Disfranchisement Convention.

When they were done, they had produced a fifty-seven-page bill chock full of a vote suppressor's dystopian fantasy. Among other things, a new photo ID provision required voters to present one of a narrow list of government-issued IDs and purposely left out IDs that were disproportionately held by Black voters and students. Early voting was cut from seventeen days to ten days before polling, and one of the two Sunday voting days—used by Black churches for "Souls-to-the-Polls" voting drives—was chopped off. Same-day registration during early voting was banned, and out-of-precinct (provisional) voting—previously counted if cast in the correct county—was banned. Preregistration for sixteen- and seventeen-year-olds was eliminated, and counties were prohibited from extending polling hours due to long lines without special permission from the state.

The final orgiastic bill was too much for the Fourth Circuit. It condemned the law for what it was—an effort to eliminate Black voters for the benefit of Republicans. "The new provisions targeted African Americans with almost surgical precision," and they were enacted by the Republican-controlled legislature "to entrench itself" by eliminating African Americans who tended to vote Democratic.[21] The decision was an important win for democracy. It also reminded Republicans to be less obvious as they went about suppressing voters.

In the first decade after *Shelby* some thirty laws that made voting more difficult went into effect in states formerly covered by Section 5.[22] With vote suppression laws being passed by Republican legislatures across the country, the difference between white and minority voting rates grew consistently after 2012, but that disparity grew twice as fast in places that had been covered by Section 5. By the 2022 midterm elections, these new laws had caused a loss of hundreds of thousands of votes from persons of color in places that had been covered by Section 5.[23]

Theoretically, after *Shelby* new voting restrictions could still be challenged under Section 2 of the Voting Rights Act, but the Supreme Court killed that option in 2021 when it upheld two devastating Arizona vote suppression laws in the infamous *Brnovich* case.[24] One of those laws made it a felony for people to collect and submit early voting ballots; the other canceled provisional ballots submitted by voters out of precinct.[25]

Brnovich fabricated a whole new set of "rules" to neuter Section 2, rules that came out of nowhere but the justices' personal hostility to voting rights. They certainly weren't based on the statute or the legislative history behind it. One of those rules gives a virtual pass to any procedure that existed in 1982 when Section 2 was amended. Another excuses any election practice that is a "mere inconvenience" or the "usual burden" of voting. That those "inconveniences" and "burdens" impact minorities much more heavily because of socioeconomic differences, occupational differences, access to childcare, and the like is now of little or no significance, even though Section 2 explicitly directs courts to weight those factors in its decision.

The facts of *Brnovich* tell an ugly story of just how radical the Supreme Court has become. Only 15 percent of Native Americans in Arizona have home mail delivery. Making it illegal for anyone other than a family member to collect early and absentee ballots and deliver them to a ballot collection site means that much of the other 85 percent of the Native American population is effectively disfranchised. That doesn't violate Section 2 anymore because such problems are just a "mere inconvenience." Even though the impact on minority voters is profound, that is permitted as a "reasonable" cost of protecting against "fraud" *even though ballot collection fraud had never occurred.* Gone was the principle that Roberts wrote in *Shelby* that "any racial discrimination in voting is too much." If he actually believed that when he wrote it—and I'm sure he didn't—he must have changed his mind. Now, quite a bit of "racial discrimination in voting" is fine with Roberts.

The hypocrisy of the Supreme Court's opinions is staggering. In *Shelby*, Section 5 was eradicated in spite of an extensive record before Congress that supported its decision to extend the law. The court ignored that record and made its own *factual* decision that the law didn't *need to be* extended. In *Brnovich*, the court did the exact opposite. There was *no evidence* that either of the Arizona statutes were necessary to protect any state interest. To the contrary, there *never* had been a problem with fraud in delivering absentee ballots or processing out-of-precinct provisional ballots. No matter. It was enough to sustain Arizona's law *restricting* voting if the state's lawyer could make up *any conceivable reason* to justify it.

In short, the Supreme Court has two diametrically opposite rules. The justification for a law designed to stop voting discrimination is closely scrutinized by the court despite an extensive legislative record that supports the law. And if five of the conservative justices don't like the law, they will decide the case based on their own version of the facts regardless of the legislative record. But if a discriminatory law is challenged because it *suppresses* voting, any reason offered will be sufficient to uphold it, even if the reason is merely hypothetical or even contradicted by the evidence. This is hypocrisy writ large.

Shelby County and *Brnovich* are radical decisions, but *Louisiana v. Callais*, an April 2026 redistricting decision, went even further. *Callais* returned voting rights law to what it had been before Section 2 was amended. Once again, voting discrimination is permitted, no matter how egregious, unless racism is proved to be the principal, driving purpose behind the law. The court eliminated the Section 2 results test by ignoring the unambiguous wording of the statute, the congressional reports that accompanied the statute, and decades of Supreme Court precedents. The court also ignored, once again, that the Constitution gives Congress—*not the court*—the power to decide what legislation is appropriate to enforce the 14th and 15th amendments.

And once again, as it did in *Shelby County*, the justices made up their own facts, divorced from reality and the legislative record, to rationalize their *personal* view of what the law should be. Section 2 as originally written is no longer necessary, said the justices, because the country has progressed so far when it comes to race. Because of that, *Callais* ruled that Black voters in Louisiana do not need a congressional district in which they are a majority; they'll do fine in districts dominated by white voters.

Were it not so serious, the court's fraudulent "facts" would be laughable. While we have progressed racially in some ways over the last 45 years, there has been little change in the voting patterns that warranted Section 2 in the first place. In 1982, very few African Americans held elected office in the South because there were few districts where Black voters were a majority. Candidates preferred by Black voters were invariably outvoted by white majorities. Today many more African Americans hold office than in 1982, but that is not because the country's voting patterns have evolved. The increase in minority representation in the South (and elsewhere) has occurred because of the proliferation of majority-minority districts, and they were created *because of the command of Section 2*. Today, African Americans are not much more likely to be elected from a majority-white district than in 1982.

Callais triggered an immediate rush in some states to eliminate majority-minority congressional districts before the 2026 midterm elections. We will see the same thing happen with state legislative districts, and in time election structures will be changed for some local governments as well, all decreasing minority representation. *Callais* permits that so long as a state can articulate any alternative nonracial justification for what it does. How far back the country will ultimately regress, only time will tell.

And yes, *Shelby County*, *Brnovich*, and *Callais* parallel the Supreme Court's awful post-Civil War destruction of congressional legislation that was enacted to remedy voting discrimination. Like the old cases, these new ones get to the result the justices want with little more than legal gibberish. As Justice Harlan said nearly a century and a half ago, "The opinions in these cases proceed . . . upon grounds entirely too narrow and artificial." While we are not heading back to the Jim Crow world that the Supreme Court saddled the country with before, the number of minority officeholders will decrease significantly, and these decisions will allow voter suppression laws that disproportionately depress non-white voting, which is just another way of stealing elections. As Justice Kagan wrote in her dissenting opinion in *Brnovich*:

A rule that throws out, each and every election, thousands of votes cast by minority citizens is a rule that can affect election outcomes. If you were a minority vote suppressor in Arizona or elsewhere, you would want that rule in your bag of tricks.

Vote suppression laws may have gotten an additional boost by *Callais*. In addition to satisfying the heavy burden *Brnovich* imposed, suppression laws might be upheld now absent additional proof of racial purpose. The potential impact of the two decisions is hard to overstate. Long-established laws like the nationwide ban on literacy tests enacted by Congress in 1970 might even be subject to a *Callais* challenge if some state tried to reinstitute a literacy test and there wasn't clear proof of a current racist motive behind the new law. While the nationwide ban was upheld by the Supreme Court[26] over half a century ago and been unquestioned since, the arch-conservative justices on the court dismiss precedents whenever they don't like them.

Today's vote suppression laws come in many flavors. Legislatures have passed new voter restrictions, changed the hours of voting, constricted early voting, limited the ways ballots can be delivered to election officials, and on and on. All of them are designed to skew the vote in favor of the Republican legislatures that enact them, but not all vote suppression comes from a legislative mandate. There are thousands of administrative decisions that affect voting in every election that can be just as oppressive and discriminatory. Voter purges are sometimes conducted on a statewide basis, at other times on a county basis only. In either case, they are constant sources of the kind of discrimination that happened in the Great Florida Purge of 2000.

The Crosscheck Program was supposed to find people who might be registered to vote in more than one place so they could be purged, but Crosscheck's work was atrocious. In North Carolina alone it identified 35,750 voters in the 2012 general election who were suspected of voting in other states as well. In fact, *only eight* were potential double voters and of those, only two people were actually shown to have voted twice—*out of the 35,750 who had been accused.*[27]

Georgia was a leader in purging votes under its "exact match" program in 2018 that disqualified new voter registrants unless every letter and number on their application matched records of the Social Security Administration or the state's database of driver licenses. Disqualified voters were given a notice with confusing information about remedying their plight and allowed forty days to navigate a Kafkaesque path. Black and Latino voters were cancelled at *ten times the rate* of white voters. Applicants who were tripped up by the exact match program were likely to live in poorer communities with lower high school graduation rates, which made correcting the cancellations more challenging. The program was stopped after a lawsuit was filed and a consent order entered.[28]

The Florida voter purge in 2000 was the first in which a state outsourced the creation of a purge list to a private company, but something more insidious is occurring in some states now. Right-wing groups challenge voters with mass lists generated from various sources. Those lists have several things in common—they are inaccurate, they are skewed to minority and Democratic voters, and they are justified with the standard mantra of "stopping voter fraud."

Most election boards rejected those challenges because they weren't what state challenge statutes were meant for, but Georgia once again led the race to the bottom. It amended its law in 2024 to allow mass challenges. State Representative Saira Draper, the most knowledgeable election expert in the General Assembly, bemoaned the legislature's latest assault on voters: "I wish we had a policy of not passing laws to placate conspiracy theorists."

The new Georgia law expands the grounds for challenging voters to include information "listed by or in a government office, data base, website, or publicly available sources derived solely from such governmental sources." Any disparity between that information and a voter's registration information will start the meat grinder to remove the voter. The insidious nature of mass challenges is that a challenge doesn't need to be successful to succeed. A registered voter who is notified of a challenge has the right to respond, but once again, people living on the margin will have a more difficult time doing so, and those are the people that are targeted by the mass challenge groups because they are vulnerable, more often Black or Brown, and vote Democratic.

In a very real sense, Georgia has delegated to private entities the power to carry out the government's responsibility for maintaining voter lists. At least in theory, states and counties are supposed to maintain voter lists without political or racial bias; the opposite is true with these third parties. Their purpose is to target Democratic voters, and that is often done by going after counties and precincts where minorities predominate.[29]

Another vote suppression tactic that has blossomed in the South since *Shelby* is closing precincts, which depresses voter participation in two ways—increased distance to the polls and longer waiting times in line. One 2016 study reviewed 381 counties in seven states that had been covered by Section 5 and found that 165 of those counties had reduced the number of polling places since *Shelby*. Arizona and Louisiana were the worst offenders of the seven. Some of the counties had reduced the number of polling locations by more than half.[30]

A detailed analysis was carried out by the *Atlanta Journal and Constitution* to determine how many voters "dropped out" because of Georgia's precinct closures between 2012 and 2018.[31] After *Shelby*, Georgia closed 214 precincts between 2012 and 2018. The number of Georgians who didn't vote *because of the time and distance to their poll* more than quadrupled by the 2018 general election compared to 2012, which means that approximately *70,000 voters did not vote* in 2018 because of precinct closures. Black voters were especially hard hit and were 20 percent more likely to miss elections because of long distances and the fact that they lived farther from their polling places, on average, than white voters. Turnout by Black voters would have been between 1.3 percent and 2.1 percent higher in the 2018 general election if they had lived comparably close to their polling places as white people—enough votes to make the difference in close elections.

The "brass ring" for Republican vote suppression today is to require voters to produce proof of citizenship.[32] Trump and his fellow travelers have manufactured hysteria about non-citizen voting as a bastard child of their all-out assault on illegal immigration. Their goal is to require documentary proof of citizenship (DPOC), which would knock out another slice of minority, young, and other Democratic voters even though they are citizens legally entitled to vote.

It's a replay of the photo-ID-voter-fraud scam that tricked Justice Stevens and Judge Posner. Republicans are again fabricating a fake issue so they can steal elections. Non-citizen voting is so rare that it's completely irrelevant to election outcomes. Speaker of the House of Representatives, Michael Johnson, parrots the party line about non-citizen voting, but the Secretary of State of Louisiana, Johnson's home state, found the opposite to be the case. Louisiana's own audit identified only seventy-nine *possible* instances of non-citizen voting out of 72 million votes cast *over the last 40 years*.[33]

North Carolina audited its 2016 general election and identified forty-one ballots that *might* have been cast by lawful permanent residents, who are non-citizens, out of a total of 4.8 million ballots, but even some of those forty-one later turned out to be citizens.[34] Utah's audit of its voter rolls found one non-citizen, but they had never voted.[35] Other state studies have similarly shown that non-citizen voting is "vanishingly rare."[36] The libertarian Cato Institute published a report responding to false claims of non-citizen voting and confirmed that voting by non-citizens is extremely rare; so rare that they "don't vote in detectable numbers."[37]

Proof of citizenship laws don't fix a problem since there isn't one, but they are perfect for doing what Republicans want—eliminating Democratic voters.

The harsh impact of DPOC laws was seen in Kansas before its law was enjoined. Many thousands of *legal voters* were stopped from casting a ballot.[38] In Arizona, a new DPOC law applies when you first register to vote. More than 31,500 registration applications were rejected for lack of documents, and community-based registration in Maricopa County dropped by nearly half. On February 25, 2025, the Ninth Circuit ruled that "many of [Arizona's] challenged provisions are unlawful measures of voter suppression" that were motivated by intentional discrimination. The case will probably be heard by the Supreme Court where all bets are off—it already granted a stay of part of the injunction.[39]

Of course, Republicans wouldn't be pushing for DPOC laws if they didn't discriminate against Democratic voters, and national studies confirm what Republicans believe. As many as 9 percent of U.S. citizen adults don't have proof-of-citizenship documents, and the share is substantially higher for Americans of color. The rate is also twice as high among citizens earning less than $40,000 per year in 2025 dollars. Getting documentary proof of citizenship can be an impossible hurdle for people without financial means, time, and mobility. The difficulty of bona fide citizens proving their citizenship status was dramatically shown when Medicaid first required DPOC in 2006. Even with the threat of losing healthcare, many thousands of American citizens were unable to get the required proof and lost their coverage.

As happened in Maricopa County, DPOC laws have an especially crushing effect on voter registration drives that register hundreds of thousands of people in a single election. Few people carry proof of citizenship documents that would allow them to register on the spot.[40]

The future of DPOC laws will depend on the Supreme Court, and several issues will be key to its decision. One of those issues, of course, will be the extent of harm to citizens and the relatively greater harm to minority citizens. The court has shown very little concern for that question so far, but the facts are so obvious maybe the court won't be so hostile. Another critical question is whether state laws like Arizona's are preempted by the terms of the National

Voter Registration Act (NVRA), at least for federal elections. If Congress passes a DPOC requirement, of course—as most Republicans would like to do—the NVRA issue would be moot.

If the Supreme Court allows DPOC laws, Republicans will have a powerful new tool to steal elections. We would then be living in a strange regime that follows the opposite of the adage that "It's better to let 100 guilty go free, than convict one innocent person." In the United States, we would be preventing *50,000 citizens* from voting to stop *one* non-citizen from voting.

10

The Next Stolen Election

Fair elections are under assault today in ways never seen before. They are attacked from all directions, by states, counties, and now the federal government. The year 2024 saw a frenzy of *hundreds* of anti-voting bills introduced in forty different states, and ten states passed nineteen different new laws to restrict voting. The cry for documentary proof of citizenship ramped up, and three states enacted new DPOC laws. As always, the justification for these hundreds of bills was to stop voter fraud. And as always, that justification itself was the real fraud.

Most of these legislative initiatives were the "usual" kinds of anti-voting restrictions discussed in previous chapters, but not all. New, more insidious ways of stealing elections have emerged from the men and women who were part of Trump's Stop the Steal fraud. As they reflected on their loss in 2020, they learned a lesson—but it was the wrong lesson. They should have realized that Trump's allegations of a "stolen election" were lies made up so he could hold on to the presidency regardless of the *fact* that he lost. They learned a different lesson. They saw Trump's claims refuted and rejected by election officials. Why not, they asked, take over those offices so they can control how elections are conducted and ballots counted? Then they would have the power to decide voter qualification challenges, restrict early voting and drop-boxes, and ultimately determine the number of votes candidates receive! If corrupt or misguided election deniers are in charge of elections, they can claim that votes from some people, selected precincts, or even an entire county are "illegal" for some "reason." They don't need real facts, evidence, or proof. Their preconceived opinions are their "facts," and they will dismiss real evidence that disproves their preconceptions as "fake."

How real is this danger? *Very!* Election thievery that was far-fetched a few years ago is now a very real threat. Stop-the-Steal cheats are trying to infiltrate state and local election administration to make the far-fetched happen. Georgia again is a national "leader." The Georgia State Election Board has a majority of Trump acolytes who passed rules just before the 2024 election to subvert fair elections. One of those rules would allow local boards to ignore their legal duty to certify an election. Instead, they would have *discretion* to "investigate," make their own "judgments" about the facts, and turn what are supposed to be routine actions into political decisions and stolen elections.

In Pennsylvania, Stop-the-Steal Republicans won seats on county commissions that have the authority to shape county election policy. In Wisconsin, Robert Spindell was a fake elector who tried to steal the 2020 election, yet he remained a member of the State Elections Commission. In North Carolina, two county board members refused to certify the 2022 election because of baseless allegations of voter fraud. When the bipartisan state commission removed them from office, the North Carolina legislature transferred the authority to appoint commission members from the governor, a Democrat, to the state auditor, a Republican. Republicans named two vote deniers to the Board of Elections in Fulton County, Georgia, home to the greatest concentration of Black voters in Georgia, and long the target of whites whose twisted thinking equates Black voters with vote fraud.

If election conspiracists and deniers control county or state election machinery, they might flip the winner of an election as Trump tried but failed to do in 2020. But they don't have to go that far to win elections. If they just declare that an election outcome is uncertain, that could be enough to steal a legislative election. The U.S. Constitution makes the Senate and the House of

Representatives the ultimate "Judge of the Elections, Returns and Qualifications of its own Members." If election deniers create a dispute over who won, or election officials simply say the results are uncertain because of "questions of fraud," "irregularities," or for any other justification, the House or Senate will decide who to seat. And there is no doubt who today's House and Senate would seat if there is any dispute.

The same scheme works on the state level. The constitutions of all fifty states have provisions like those in the U.S. Constitution. State legislatures are the ultimate judges of the elections of their members. If there's a dispute over who won, or if election officials simply say the result is uncertain, the state house or senate has the authority to determine the winner.

The rule passed by the Georgia Election Board did not go into effect because the Georgia Supreme Court said it was not authorized by the General Assembly, but there is a move now by adamant election deniers to enact it as law. And the Supreme Court's decision didn't slow the anti-voter members who control the board. Their latest causes are eliminating drop-box voting, withdrawing the state from the bipartisan ERIC database that is used to confirm voter information (because Trump doesn't like it), and replacing touch screen voting with paper ballots—forgetting that paper ballots were abandoned years ago because many votes were lost when ballots were not marked as clearly as the scanners required.

And so the cult of conspiracies metastasizes in state after state as Trumpian soldiers march on in their holy war of illusion. When it ends—which it will, even if consumed in its own fire—what will our elections look like?

Historically, federal legislation has made voter registration and casting ballots more accessible. That was particularly true in the South, of course, where voting discrimination was pervasive. But the paradigm of progress through federal voting laws is over for now. The Republican majorities in the House and Senate want to make voting less accessible, and for the first time ever, the White House is occupied by a man who is rabid about restricting voting. If Congress and the president have their way, restrictive legislation modeled after the worst state laws will be enacted on the federal level.

Since laws like that would be doing the opposite of what Congress *should* be doing, wouldn't they be unconstitutional? Yes, but the Supreme Court has the last word, and the current court has made it clear that they are in on the game. So long as Congress simply mouths the words "vote fraud," the Supreme Court will likely uphold any restriction Congress passes.

Trump came frighteningly close to stealing the 2020 presidential election. He told the attorney general to seize election equipment so he could claim to have "proof" that reported vote totals were wrong; to file bogus lawsuits challenging the results in the battleground states so he could manipulate their electoral votes; and to "just say the election is corrupt and leave the rest to [himself] and Republican congressmen." Trump tried to get states to falsify their returns, and on January 6, he tried to corrupt the electoral vote count by unleashing his personal militia on the Capitol.

In each instance, Trump's effort to steal the election failed only because the attorney general, the vice president, or another official said "No." We live in a different world today. Trump said he made a mistake in his first term by appointing "disloyal" people to office, and he wouldn't make that mistake again. The key requirement for a position in the Trump II government is *loyalty to Trump*. Loyalty to the American people and the U.S. Constitution? Irrelevant.

Pam Bondi was appointed attorney general because of her lack of principle and loyalty to Donald Trump. Her successor will surely be someone cut from the same cloth.

Chris Wray, appointed by Trump as director of the FBI in 2017, testified before a Senate committee that the January 6 rioters were "right-wing domestic terrorists." He also testified that the greatest danger in America are men like the Proud Boys who attacked the Capitol on Trump's orders, men and some women are "standing by," waiting for Trump to call on them again more empowered than ever with 1,500 pardons in their pockets. Trump said he would replace Wray with Kash Patel. The problem with Wray? He was honest.

Kash Patel is a right-wing conspiracy theorist who has pedaled false claims about the 2020 election, QAnon conspiracies, and Covid-19 vaccines. His qualification? Absolute loyalty to Donald Trump. Patel would never say that right-wing groups are a danger no matter what the truth. He understands his job is to bolster Trump's lies and pursue Trump's enemies.

And the Secretary of Defense? *Fox News* talking head Pete Hegseth, who suffers the same disability as Bondi and Patel. There is no Mark Esper or James Mattis now, nor any of the previous Secretaries of Defense, *all* of whom published a joint op-ed in the *Washington Post* on January 3, 2021, that said, "Hell no!" when Trump advisers recommended martial law to steal the 2020 election.

Ed Martin is a right-wing political operative so extreme that even the Republican rubber-stamp Senate wouldn't confirm him as U.S. attorney for the District of Columbia. But in his short stint as the temporary U.S. attorney there, Martin cleaned house for Trump and fired all the career prosecutors who had anything to do with the Trump investigation and indictment.

In doublespeak that would make George Orwell blush, Trump named Martin the director of the DOJ's Weaponization Working Group, ostensibly created to look into past misuse of the department for political purposes, but actually designed to do exactly what it was supposed to eradicate—harass, target, investigate, and indict political "enemies." The targets? Anyone who has ever criticized Trump. Martin was perfect for the job, a Trump loyalist who showed that facts don't get in his way as a leader in the Stop-the-Steal scam. If a prosecutor said there was no basis to indict a Trump target? No problem. Fire the prosecutor.

Trump has such a bizarre, insatiable need for attention and flattery that he has to post constantly on social media, attacking his enemies, and telling his followers how great he is. When he told Bondi to indict his enemies, he had to broadcast it on social media. "Pam," Trump posted, "We can't delay any longer, it's killing our reputation and credibility. They impeached me twice, and indicted me (5 times!), OVER NOTHING. JUSTICE MUST BE SERVED, NOW!!!"[1]

When U.S. Attorney Erik Siebert was forced out because he didn't think there were grounds to indict James Comey, Trump appointed Lindsey Halligan to replace him. Her experience was with insurance law before she became part of the team that represented Trump over his removal of classified documents. As soon as Halligan took office, prosecutors told her the evidence was insufficient to justify prosecution. No problem. She ignored the evidence and did what Trump wanted—indicted Comey on September 25, 2025.

It didn't take long for Halligan to bring her second political indictment. In early October 2025 she brought an indictment against New York Attorney General Letitia James. The indictment read "mortgage fraud." Her real crime? Bringing a successful fraud case against Trump.

Rarely does a week go by that Trump doesn't tell the DOJ to go after someone else he doesn't like. John Bolton's memoir told the truth about Trump's incompetence. His indictment followed. Soon after, Trump told the press, flanked by Bondi, Patel, and Bondi's chief deputy, Todd Blanche, about other "bad guys" who needed investigated and indicted:

> Deranged Jack Smith, in my opinion, is a criminal . . . His interviewer was Weissmann—I hope they're going to look into Weissmann, too—Weissmann's a bad guy . . . And he had somebody, Lisa [Monaco, deputy attorney general under Merrick Garland], who was his puppet, worked in the office, really, as the top person. I think she should be looked at very strongly.[2]

Their crimes? Trying to bring Trump to justice for attempting to steal the 2020 election.

Trump posted on Truth Social that George Soros and his son should be indicted and jailed as racketeers. Their support of progressive causes drives Trump crazy. Trump's post was absurd, but a lawyer in the office of the deputy attorney general immediately directed DOJ offices around the country to go after Soros.[3] Whether they indict Soros or not, the mere threat of an investigation accomplishes Trump's goal—scaring people away from supporting causes that Trump doesn't like. Trump has used threats and bullying his whole life. They are as much a part of his being as breathing. He knows how they work. Indicting a few people, even if there's no conviction, will mute others.

When Nixon talked about using "the power" of the DOJ against his enemies, what he imagined was child's play compared to what Trump II is doing. FCC Chairman Brendan Carr has threatened to use federal licensing power to punish media companies that don't toe the Trump line.[4] The right of free speech is ignored—unless the speech comes from the far right. Trump admits that he wants the FCC to go after stations that are unfriendly to him.[5] Universities that irritate Trump are threatened with losing research funds that have been a major source for the United States' competitive edge. He has attacked law firms whose lawyers investigated him. Some of those firms promised Trump huge payments in the form of legal work to get him to back off, payments that reeked of extortion. In a single week, he said that protesters who yelled at him should be prosecuted as racketeers; that comics who criticize him should be fired; and that TV broadcasters who criticize him should be shut down. He also sued the *New York Times* for damaging his "reputation." He has said criticizing him should be illegal.[6]

Trump has sent the National Guard into Democratic cities *because* they are Democratic. He wants to create chaos and fear. When Trump was sued to stop the National Guard invasion of Illinois, the judge asked the DOJ lawyer if it would be legal for Trump to send troops to subdue disorder *if the president had intentionally caused the trouble to start with?* The attorney answered "yes" and said Trump's decision could not be challenged for any reason. The Seventh Circuit disagreed. Federal law allows a president to federalize National Guard troops if there is a "rebellion," but "[p]olitical opposition is not rebellion."[7]

For Trump, the law has never been more than something to be manipulated and abused to serve his ends. Trump I proved that conclusively, and the Supreme Court's stupefying presidential immunity decision has freed him to do whatever he wants during his second term as president. He no longer has any reason to fear being called to account for any crimes he commits while in office.[8]

Trump insists that Republican states ratchet up their gerrymanders to cancel out voter preferences and win more seats in Congress. He has converted the DOJ voting rights division into the opposite of what it's supposed to be. Now it has become the *anti*-voting rights division and intervenes in cases *in favor* of vote suppressors and in defense of discrimination. Trump has appointed election deniers to positions that are supposed to protect election integrity, but these are people whose experience is in pushing falsehoods to steal elections. Heather Honey, a prominent election denier, is the deputy assistant secretary for Election Integrity in the Department of Homeland Security. Honey was a key player in the bogus "election audit" by Arizona Republicans after the 2020 election. Cleta Mitchell—who was on Trump's phone call when he tried to make Secretary of State Raffensperger falsify Georgia's 2020 returns—is on the board of advisors for the Election Assistance Commission that is supposed to help states with voting procedures and federal requirements.

The FBI joined the fanatical election deniers on the Georgia Election Board who parrot Trump's claim that the state's 2020 electoral votes were "stolen." The locus of their imagined "steal," of course, is Fulton County with its large number of predominantly Black Democratic voters. The FBI in 2026 seized the county's old election records, ignoring the fact that every claim of fraud had previously been investigated and disproven by the FBI itself, the U.S. Attorney's office in Atlanta, Georgia's Republican Secretary of State, and the Georgia GBI. What was Trump's game? The same ploy he admitted to in 2020—to have the DOJ "just *say* the election was corrupt," and he would "take care of the rest." The truth was irrelevant.

The Trump administration is demanding that states turn over detailed information about their registered voters. When Kobach tried the same thing on behalf of Trump's so-called Commission on Election Integrity in 2017, states exploded in opposition. At least forty-four states, red as well as blue, refused to provide the information which Trump said the commission needed to track down fraud and the "millions" of illegal votes he falsely said were cast in the 2016 election.[9]

Trump II is going after state voter records now with a vengeance—including non-public data like voter social security numbers—and the DOJ is suing Democratic states that refuse to comply.[10] Why do Trump and Republican operatives want that information? Simple. Just think of the ways it can be used to steal elections, and you'll know why they want it.

First, they will say they have "reviewed" all the data and it validates their past claims of voter fraud and non-citizens voting. When they are asked for the underlying data so it can be examined to expose their lies, they will say that can't be done because it would violate voter privacy. Second, they will misrepresent the data to justify new kinds of voter suppression laws. Third, they will misuse the data to justify drawing discriminatory districts. Fourth, they will make bogus challenges to state voter lists like those that have been brought by private anti-voter groups. Fifth, they will have all the data at the ready to make false claims of election fraud when Republicans lose elections. Think of the Stop-the-Steal falsehoods backed up by pseudo-"expert" testimony using this data, and you will see what election fights can look like in the future.

The next time Trump claims election fraud, Patel's FBI will back him up. So will whoever Trump appoints as attorney general.. The facts won't matter to them. When Trump tells the DOJ to seize election equipment, who will stop him now? When there is a Trump-led chorus calling for martial law in one state or another, will this Supreme Court agree with the Seventh Circuit that "political opposition is not a rebellion" that allows Trump to call out the

National Guard? If Trump wants to declare martial law, will Secretary of Defense Hegseth do what all of his predecessors did and say "no"?

Trump II has already caused a tectonic shift in the world of elections, and more is coming. He said in 2024 that his "beautiful Christians . . . wouldn't have to vote again" if they elected him. The Constitution is clear that no one can serve as president more than two terms. Still, there is the noise of Trump somehow having a third term. Stephen Bannon has said, "Trump is going to be president in '28, and people ought to just get accommodated with that."[11] Bannon also said before the 2020 election that Trump would declare victory and try to hold on no matter what the vote. As preposterous as that sounded, Bannon was right.

Other than in the farthest fringes, talk of a three-term Trump is just part of Trump being a chaos agent. So much nonsense comes from him that people can't respond to all that he does that is bad for middle class and poor Americans, bad for the country's future, and bad for the world as a whole—to say nothing of the massive corruption that shapes nearly everything he touches as president.[12] Before people can respond to one thing, he has already done three more things just as offensive or worse. Trump is a master distracter.

Could the Supreme Court "get around" the constitutional prohibition on his serving again? If he tried the Putin–Medvedev ploy and ran as Vance's vice-president with the understanding Trump would be in control, would the Supreme Court rule that he couldn't be on the ballot? Or would the Republicans on the court do something like they did when Colorado tried to exclude Trump from the ballot because he had "engaged in an insurrection" and was therefore disqualified from office under the express terms of the Fourteenth Amendment?[13] Granted, the situations are different, but the majority's ruling in the Colorado case that the constitutional barrier was "ineffective" because Congress hadn't passed legislation to implement it was nonsense, made up just to be sure Trump's insurrectionist history couldn't be used to disqualify him. Might the Supreme Court do something equally disingenuous to "get around" the eligibility limit for a vice president? All very, very far-fetched, but these are far-fetched times.

William G. Young is a federal judge appointed by Ronald Reagan who has been presiding over a case which has caused him to ask whether the First Amendment can survive the Trump presidency.[14] The Secretary of State Marco Rubio had ordered the arrest and deportation of people lawfully in this country *solely* because they exercised their First Amendment right to speak out on Palestine in a way that President Trump did not like. The government "targeted a few for speaking out and then . . . publicly deported them with the goal of . . . terrorizing similarly situated non-citizen (and other) pro-Palestinians into silence." ICE agents wore masks while they rounded up people "*for a single reason—to terrorize Americans into quiescence.*" Judge Young anguished over the consequences of what the government was doing.

> Perhaps we're now afraid to stick our necks out. If the distinguished Homeland Security intelligence agency can be weaponized to squelch the free speech rights of a small, hapless group of non-citizens in our midst, so too can the Federal Home Loan Mortgage Corporation, and the audit divisions of the I.R.S. and the Social Security Administration be unconstitutionally weaponized against the President's ever growing list of "enemies" or opponents he "hates," notwithstanding that political persecution is anathema to our Constitution and everything for which America stands.

The Judge expressly addressed Trump's personal culpability:

> The President wholeheartedly supported [the ICE operation], making many individual case specific comments (some quite cruel) that demonstrate he has been fully briefed. Such conduct, of course, violates his sacred oath to "faithfully execute the Office of President of the United States, and . . . to the best of [his] Ability, preserve, protect and defend the Constitution of the United States," U.S. Const. art. II, § 1, cl. 8, by ignoring the Constitution's command that the President "take Care that the Laws be faithfully executed."

In normal times, the remedy for violating the Constitution poses little question because the government follows the orders of its courts. But these are not normal times, Young wrote, not with Trump as president. Young feared the government would continue to ignore the Constitution because the Department of Justice would do what Trump wants regardless of the law.

Young concluded his 161-page order with thoughts on the state of the country and the First Amendment. He first quoted from the famous words of Ronald Reagan: "*Freedom is a fragile thing and it's never more than one generation away from extinction. It is not ours by way of inheritance; it must be fought for and defended constantly by each generation, for it comes only once to a people.*"

Judge Young then went on to explain what those words meant both to him and to Donald Trump:

> I first heard these words of President Reagan's back in 2007 when my son quoted them in the Law Day celebration speech at the Norfolk Superior Court. I was deeply moved and hold these words before me as I discharge judicial duties. As I've read and re-read the record in this case, listened widely, and reflected extensively, I've come to believe that President Trump truly understands and appreciates the full import of President Reagan's inspiring message—yet I fear he has drawn from it a darker, more cynical message. I fear President Trump believes the American people are so divided that today they will **not** stand up, fight for, and defend our most precious constitutional values so long as they are lulled into thinking their own personal interests are not affected.
>
> Is he correct?

Judge Young's question arose in a First Amendment case, but it applies equally to the country's elections. Has President Trump drawn from the words of Ronald Reagan the "dark, cynical message" that he can get away with subverting our elections? Can he misuse the powers of the government to achieve his illicit aims? He is explicit about what those aims are—to ensure that "Republicans will control Congress for the next fifty years." And he is remarkably candid about how he believes he can sabotage fair elections—by gerrymandering, making voting much more difficult, and by outright seizing the election machinery of the states. Everything he is doing that touches on voting serves his one overriding goal: the election of Republicans who will allow him to do whatever he wants as president. What the people might want and who they might elect if allowed to vote freely in fair elections is of no concern.

What President Trump wants is clear, but is he right that people "will not stand up, fight for, and defend" fair elections? The survival of our constitutional values and the survival of fair elections depend on us, the people. If Trump's cynical view is right and we don't *fight* to keep our freedoms, then Trump, feckless Republican legislators, and their post-truth crusaders will sweep those freedoms away. And once gone, they will be hard to recover because *freedom comes only once to a people.*

NOTES

1 Tilden–Hayes and the Stolen Presidency of 1876

1 Robert G. Ingersoll, "Indianapolis Speech Delivered to the Veteran Soldiers of the Rebellion, 1876," *THESECULARWEB*, https://infidels.org/library/historical/robert-ingersoll-indianapolis-speech76/.

2 Jerome Sternstein, "The Sickles Memorandum: Another Look at the Hayes–Tilden Election-Night Conspiracy," *Journal of Southern History* (August 1966): 355.

3 *Florida ex rel. Drew vs McLin*, 16 FL. 17 (1876).

4 *New Orleans Democrat*, July 5, 1876, 2.

5 Ella Lonn, *Reconstruction in Louisiana After 1868* (New York, G.P. Putnam's Sons 1918), 427.

6 Lonn, *Reconstruction in Louisiana After 1868*, 429.

7 House Misc. Doc., 44 Cong., 2 Sess., No. 34, Part i., 88, quoted in Lonn, *Reconstruction in Louisiana After 1868*, 455, n. 5.

8 House Misc. Doc., 44 Cong., 2 Sess., No. 42, 180, quoted in Lonn, *Reconstruction in Louisiana After 1868*, 458–9.

9 Lonn, *Reconstruction in Louisiana After 1868*, 460.

10 House Rept., 44 Cong., 2 Sess., No. 156, Part i., 9, quoted in Lonn, *Reconstruction in Louisiana After 1868*, 467–8.

11 C. Vann Woodward, *Reunion and Reaction: The Compromise of 1877 and the End of Reconstruction* (New York, Oxford University Press 1966), 68–121.

12 "Samuel Tilden Concedes the 1876 Election to Hayes," *New York Herald*, June 13, 1877, 3, https://www.rbhayes.org/hayes/1876-presidential-concession-speech/.

2 When Georgia had Three Governors

1 *Congressional Record*, March 23, 1900, 56th Congress, first session, 3223, line 33, part 5, page S4972.

2 Neil R. McMillen, *The Citizens' Council: Organized Resistance to the Second Reconstruction, 1954–64* (Urbana: University of Illinois Press, 1994), 3.

3 William Anderson, *The Wild Man From Sugar Creek: The Political Career of Eugene Talmadge* (Baton Rouge: Louisiana State University Press, 1975), 30.

4 *Atlanta Constitution*, September 18, 1934, 1; Anderson, *The Wild Man From Sugar Creek*, 110–11.

5 *Atlanta Constitution* August 6, 1936, 6.

6 *Atlanta Constitution*, August 30, 1936, 14.

7 *Chapman vs King*, 154 F.2d 460 (1946).

8 *Atlanta Constitution*, June 7, 1946, 4.

9 *Atlanta Constitution*, June 23, 1946; *Atlanta Daily World*, July 5, 1946.

10 *Macon Telegraph*, July 19, 1946, 1.

11 *Atlanta Constitution*, July 16, 1946, 10.

12 *Fredericksburg Free Lance-Star*, July 12, 1946, 4.

13 *Atlanta Daily World*, July 19, 1946, 6.

14 *Atlanta Constitution*, February 13, 1947, 10.

15 *Atlanta Journal*, March 2, 1947, 1.

16 *Atlanta Journal*, March 2, 1947, 10.

17 Herman E. Talmadge, "Interview by Mel Steely and Dan Wagner, September 24, 1985," https://kaltura.uga.edu/media/t/1_rfxstnl7.

18 *Atlanta Journal*, January 15, 1947.

19 *New York Times*, January 16, 1947.

20 *Atlanta Constitution*, January 22, 1947.

21 *Time Magazine*, February 3, 1947, https://time.com/archive/6822484/georgia-double-trouble/.

22 *Atlanta Journal*, March 2, 1947, 1.

3 Lyndon Johnson—Two Stolen Elections on the Way to the Presidency

1 John Connally, Oral History, June 30, 1988, LBJ Library, 2.

2 Robert A. Caro, *The Path to Power* (New York: Vintage Books 1980), 409.

3 Robert W. Murphey, Oral History, LBJ Library, 10–11.

4 Archie Parr, Oral History, August 23, 1984, LBJ Library, 8,

5 J. P. McEvoy, "I've Got that Million Dollar Smile," *Texas Weekly*, July 2, 1938.

6 *American-Statesman*, June 22, 1941, 4.

7 *American-Statesman*, June 30, 1941, 1.

8 Sam D. W. Low, Oral History, LBJ Library, 9–10.

9 Brian Sweany, "Texas History," *Texas Monthly*, February 2006, 101.

10 Connally, Oral History, 12–14.

11 Connally, Oral History, 8.

12 Connally, Oral History, 27.

13 George Norris Green, *The Establishment in Texas Politics: The Primitive Years, 1938–1957* (Norman: University of Oklahoma Press, 1984), 114.

14 *Dallas Morning News*, August 31, 1948

15 Robert A. Caro, *Means of Ascent* (New York: Vintage Books, 1990), 343.

16 Caro, *Means of Ascent*, 348.

17 John Connally, Interview, November 28, 1969, LBJ Library, 41.

18 Josh Groce, Interview, August 3, 1983, LBJ Library, 9.

19 Groce, Interview, 9.

20 Abe Fortas, Interview, August 14, 1969, LBJ Library, 5–6.

21 Fortas, Interview, 5–6.

22 Fortas, Interview, 6–7.

23 *Johnson vs. Stevenson*, 335 U.S. 801 (1948).

24 *Johnson vs. Stevenson*, 170 F.2d 108 (5th Cir. 1948).

4 Jimmy Carter's 1962 Senate Race Almost Stole his Presidency

1 Jimmy Carter, *Turning Point* (New York: Times Books, 1992), 41.

2 *Atlanta Constitution*, September 28, 1962, pg. 1

3 *Atlanta Constitution*, October 6, 1962, pg. 11.

4 Carter, *Turning Point*, 52–3.

5 Carter, *Turning Point*, 84.

6 Carter, *Turning Point*, 91.

7 Carter, *Turning Point*, 92.

8 Carter, *Turning Point*, 166.

9 Carter, *Turning Point*, 167.

10 Carter, *Turning Point*, 201.

5 Two Centuries of Voter Suppression

1 James Madison in Max Farrand (ed.), *The Records of The Federal Convention of 1787, Vol. II* (New Haven, CT: Yale University Press, 1911), 203–4.

2 "Expansion of Rights and Liberties—The Right of Suffrage," in *The Charters of Freedom*, National Archives, http://www.archives.gov/exhibits/charters/charters_of_freedom_13.html.

3 *In re Opinion of the Justices*, 3 R.I. 299, 301 (1854).

4 Rory Raven, *The Dorr War* (London: The History Press, 2010), 19.

5 Stanley L. Engerman and Kenneth L. Sokoloff, "The Evolution of Suffrage Institutions in the New World," *65 Journal of Economic History* (2005): 891, 907, https://web.archive.org/web/20180722015654id_/http://tuvalu.santafe.edu/events/workshops/images/d/d3/TheEvolSuffrage.pdf.

6 *Cipriano vs City of Houma*, 395 US 701 (1969); *City of Phoenix vs. Kolodziejski*, 410 US 719 (1973).

7 1776 Const. of New Jersey, Dept. of Archives, State of New Jersey, https://www.nj.gov/state/archives/docconst76.html#page3.

8 Edward Turner, "Women's Suffrage in New Jersey 1790 to 1807," *Smith College Studies in History* 1, no. 4 (1916): 181–4, https://dn790000.ca.archive.org/0/items/womenssuffragein00turnuoft/womenssuffragein00turnuoft.pdf.

9 *Bradwell vs. Illinois*, 83 U.S. 130 (1872).

10 Maud Wood Park, "The Woman Movement in Review," in *Independent Woman*, June 1930, 236, referenced in Wikipedia, *Women's Suffrage in Wyoming*.

11 "Five Absurd Reasons Women were Denied the Vote," *Britannica*, https://www.britannica.com/video/Five-reasons-why-people-thought-women-shouldnt-vote-womens-suffrage/-247523.

12 Carrie Chapman Catt and Nettie Rogers Shuler, *Woman Suffrage and Politics: The Inner Story of the Suffrage Movement* (New York: Charles Scribner's Sons 1923; republished by Dover in 2020), 438–9.

13 *Slaughter-House Cases*, 83 U.S. 36, 71 (1873).

14 Lou Falkner Williams, *The Great South Carolina Ku Klux Klan Trials, 1871–1872* (Athens: University of Georgia Press, 1966).

15 *United States vs. Cruikshank*, 92 U.S. 542 (1875).

16 109 U.S. 3 (1883).

17 163 U.S. 537 (1896).

18 A majority of the justices expressed their disagreement with the *Civil Rights Cases* and its narrow interpretation of Congress' power to implement the 14th Amendment in *United States vs. Guest*, 383 U.S. 745 (1966) (concurring opinions joined by Clark, Warren, Brennan, Black, Douglas, and Fortas). However, the court soon became much more hostile to civil rights with Nixon's appointments so that what the concurring justices wrote in the *Guest* case never became a controlling majority opinion.

19 Letter from Bradley to Woods, quoted in F. Ugarte, "Reconstruction Redux: Rehnquist, Morrison, and the Civil Rights Cases," *Harvard Civil Rights–Civil Liberties Law Review* 481 (2006): 41.

20 170 U.S. 213 (1898).

21 *Ratliff vs Beale*, 74 Miss. 247, 20 So. 865, 868 (1896).

22 189 U.S. 475 (1903).

23 J. Morgan Kousser, *The Shipping of Southern Politics* (New Haven, CT: Yale University Press, 1974), 15, 61.

24 *Grovey vs. Townsend*, 295 U.S. 45 (1935).

25 *Smith vs. Allright*, 321 U.S. 649 (1944).

26 *Harper vs. Virginia*, 383 U.S. 663, 670 (1966), overruling *Breedlove vs. Suttles*, 302 U.S. 277 (1937).

27 446 U.S. 55 (1980).

28 U.S. Senate, Committee on the Judiciary, *Voting Rights Act Extension, Report No. 97-1417*, May 25 1982.

6 The Bush–Gore Election: A Bloodless Coup

1 Lisa Getter, "Florida Net too Wide in Purge of Voter Polls," *Los Angeles Times*, May 21, 2001.

2 Greg Palast, *The Best Democracy Money Can Buy* (London: Pluto Press, 2002), 33–4.

3 *Schlenther vs. Dept of State*, 743 So.2d 536, 537 (Fla. Ct. App., 2nd Dist. 1998).

4 Palast, *The Best Democracy Money Can Buy*, 25.

5 Palast, *The Best Democracy Money Can Buy*, 28.

6 U.S. Commission on Civil Rights, *Voting Irregularities in Florida During the 2000 Presidential Election* (2001), 4–8.

7 Getter, "Florida Net too Wide."

8 Jake Trapper, *Down & Dirty: The Plot to Steal the Presidency* (New York: Little, Brown and Company, 2001), 310.

9 Tapper, *Down & Dirty*, 20.

10 *Today Show*, NBC, November 9, 2000 https://web.archive.org/web/20200914204811/https://www.presidency.ucsb.edu/documents/presidential-documents-archive-guidebook/documents-related-the-2000-election-dispute-17.

11 Tapper, *Down & Dirty*, 73–4.

12 *Today Show*, November 9, 2000, https://web.archive.org/web/20200914204811/https://www.presidency.ucsb.edu/documents/presidential-documents-archive-guidebook/documents-related-the-2000-election-dispute-17.

13 Joel Engelhardt and Scott McCabe, "Ballot Confusion Cost Gore 6,600 Votes," *Palm Beach Post*, March 11, 2001.

14 U.S. Commission on Civil Rights, *Voting Irregularities in Florida During the 2000 Presidential Election*, 12–19.

15 Jeffrey Tobin, *Too Close to Call* (New York: Random House Trade Paperbacks 2001), 86.

16 *Siegel vs. LePore*, 120 F.Supp.2d 1041 (S.D. Fla. 2000).

7 Drawing Districts to Win and Screw the Other Guy

1 *MacDougall vs. Green*, 335 U.S. 281, 284 (1948)

2 *Colegrove vs. Green*, 328 U.S. 549 (1946).

3 "Reapportionment and party realignment in the American States," University of Pennsylvania, Law School, *The Free Library* (2004), https://www.thefreelibrary.com/Reapportionment+and+party+realignment+in+the+American+States.-a0134168409.

4 Andrew Hacker, *Congressional Districting* (Washington: Brookings Institution 1963), 23.

5 *Baker vs. Carr*, 369 U.S. 186 (1962).

6 "A Conversation with Earl Warren" McClatchy Broadcasting (1969), https://archive.org/details/casacsh_000016.

7 *Wesberry vs. Sanders*, 376 U.S. 1 (1964).

8 *Salyer Land Co. vs. Tulare Water Storage District*, 410 U.S. 719 (1973).

9 Erick Trickey, "Where Did the Term 'Gerrymander' Come From?" *Smithsonian Magazine*, July 2017, https://www.smithsonianmag.com/history/where-did-term-gerrymander-come-180964118/.

10 John Lynch, *The Facts of Reconstruction* (New York: Neale Publishing Co., 1913), 74–80.

11 *Busbee vs. Smith*, 549 F. Supp. 494, 500 (D.D.C. 1982), affirmed, 459 U.S. 1166 (1983).

12 *Busbee vs. Smith*, 501.

13 *Georgia vs. Ashcroft*, 539 U.S. 461 (2003).

14 *Davis vs. Bandemer*, 478 U.S. 109 (1986).

15 *Rucho vs. Common Cause*, 588 U.S. 684 (2019).

16 Sam Wang, "The Great Gerrymander of 2012," *New York Times*, February 2, 2013.

17 Alex Keena, Michael Latner, Anthony J. McGann and Charles Anthony Smith, *Gerrymandering the States: Partisanship, Race and the Transformation of American Federalism* (New York: Cambridge University Press, 2021), 9–11; Anthony J. McGann, Charles Anthony Smith, Michael Latner, and Alex Keena, *Gerrymandering in America: The House of Representatives, the Supreme Court, and the Future of Popular Sovereignty* (New York: Cambridge University Press, 2016), 4, 88–90.

18 Michael Li et al., "How Gerrymandering Tilts the Race for the House," September 24, 2024, *Brennan Center for Justice*, https://www.brennancenter.org/our-work/research-reports/how-gerrymandering-tilts-2024-race-house.

19 *League of Women Voters vs. Utah State Legislature*, 2025 UT 39, 579 P.3d 287 (2025).

20 *Malliotakis vs. Williams*, 607 U. S. ____ (2026).

21 *League of United Latin American Citizens vs. Abbott*, F. Supp. 3d (W.D. Tex)(three-judge court), order stayed, 607 U.S. (2025).

22 *Harper vs. Hall*, 380 N.C. 317 (2022), overruled, 384 N.C. 292 (2023).

23 *League of Women Voters vs. Detzner*, 172 So.3d 363, 369 (2015).

24 *Black Voters Matter vs. Secretary of State*, 415 So.3d 180 (2025).

25 Jacob Wendler, "Republicans notch redistricting win in Ohio—but it could have been worse for Democrats," *Politico*, October 31, 2025, https://www.politico.com/news/2025/10/31/ohio-redistricting-gerrymander-new-map-00631254.

26 377 U.S. 533, 562 (1964).

8 Stop the Steal!

1 *Final Report of the Select Committee to Investigate the January 6th Attack on the United States Capitol*, H. Rep. No. 117-663, 3 (hereinafter, *Select Report*).

2 Mark T. Esper, interview on MSNBC's *Morning Joe*, May 2022, quoted at https://www.marktesper.com/esper-says-trump-in-unfit?utm_source=chatgpt.com.

3 https://thehill.com/homenews/news/521507-john-kelly-called-trump-the-most-flawed-person-hes-ever-met-report/.

4 Conor Finnegan, "Bolton: Trump's not 'fit for office,' doesn't have 'competence to carry out the job,'" *ABC News*, June 18, 2020, https://abcnews.go.com/Politics/bolton-trumps-fit-office-competence-carry-job/story?id=71311306&utm_source=chatgpt.com.

5 Atja Vujić, *Trump's Former Press Secretary Skewered Him at the DNC*, August 21, 2024, https://www.thecut.com/article/what-did-stephanie-grisham-say-about-trump-at-the-dnc.html?utm_source=chatgpt.com.

6 Nick Evans, "Vance Wondered Whether Trump was 'America's Hitler,'" *Ohio Capital Journal*, April 19, 2022, https://ohiocapitaljournal.com/2022/04/19/americas-hitler-old-j-d-vance-message-turns-up-in-heated-senate-primary/.

7 Trump's close relationship with Cohn has been documented many times. Cohn, who died in 1986, said Trump called him daily for advice. See, e.g., Marie Brenner, "Deal with the Devil," *Vanity Fair*, August 2017; Marcus Baram, "Eavesdropping on Roy Cohn and Donald Trump," *New Yorker*, April 14, 2017, https://www.newyorker.com/news/news-desk/eavesdropping-on-roy-cohn-and-donald-trump?utm_source=chatgpt.com; Maggie Haberman, *Confidence Man: The Making of Donald Trump and the Breaking of America* (New York: Penguin Press, 2022); Michael Kranish and Marc Fisher, *Trump Revealed: the Definitive Biography of the 45th President* (New York: Scribner, 2016). Their relationship is dramatized in Ali Abassi (Dir.), *The Apprentice*, Scythia Films, 2024.

8 Trump's trail of baseless allegations made to harass people is lengthy. One of many examples is the case he filed in 2022 against Hillary Clinton, the Democratic National Committee, and others, alleging that they "maliciously conspired to weave a false narrative that [Trump] was colluding with [Russia]" during the 2016 presidential election. He asked for $72 million in damages. The case was dismissed as frivolous and Trump and his attorney were then sanctioned. The judge wrote: "Here, we are confronted with a lawsuit that should never have been filed, which was completely frivolous, both factually and legally, and which was brought in bad faith for an improper purpose. Mr. Trump is a prolific and sophisticated litigant who is repeatedly using the courts to seek revenge on political adversaries. He is the mastermind of strategic abuse of the judicial process, and he cannot be seen as a litigant blindly following the advice of a lawyer. He knew full well the impact of his actions . . . As such, I find that sanctions should be imposed upon Mr. Trump and his lead counsel, Ms. Habba". *Trump vs. Clinton*, 653 F.Supp.3d 1198 (M.D. Fla. 2023), affirmed in relevant parts, 161 F.4th 671 (11th Cir. 2025).

9 *Select Report*, 201.

10 *Select Report*, 201–2.

11 *Select Report*, 219.

12 *Select Report*, 9.

13 *Select Report*, 9

14 *Select Report*, 9.

15 *Select Report*, 10–11.

16 *Select Report*, 11.

17 *Select Report*, 375.

18 *Select Report*, 15.

19 *Bowyer vs. Ducey*, 506 F.Supp.3d 699 (D. Ariz. 2020).

20 *King vs. Whitmer*, 505 F.Supp.3d 720 (E.D. Mich. 2020).

21 *King vs. Whitmer, supra*, Order of August 25, 2021, Select Report, 18.

22 *Donald J. Trump for President, Inc. vs. Secretary of Pennsylvania*, 830 Fed. Appx. 377 (3rd Cir. 2020).

23 *Law vs. Whitmer*, 136 Nev. 840, 477 P.3d 1124 (2020).

24 *Select Report*, 210.

25 Audio recording and transcript of Trump call to Raffensperger, January 2, 2021, https://www.cnn.com/2021/01/03/politics/trump-brad-raffensperger-phone-call-transcript.

26 Audio recording and transcript of Trump call to Raffensperger.

27 https://www.youtube.com/watch?v=7X3KzL6xbjU.

28 *Select Report*, 303.

29 *Select Report*, 305.

30 *Select Report*, 27–8.

31 *Select Report*, 277.

32 *Select Report*, 376–7.

33 *Select Report*, 380.

34 *Select Report*, 386.

35 *Select Report*, 386.

36 *Select Report*, 392.

37 *Select Report*, 396.

38 *Select Report*, 399.

39 *Select Report*, 400–1.

40 *Select Report*, 507.

41 *Select Report*, 499.

42 *Select Report*, 529.

43 *Select Report*, 527.

44 *Select Report*, 500–1.

45 *Select Report*, 531.

46 *Select Report*, 442.

47 *Select Report*, 450–3.

48 Bob Woodward and Robert Costa, *Peril* (New York: Simon & Schuster, 2021), 229.

49 *Select Report*, 538.

50 *Select Report*, 585.

51 *Select Report*, 596.

52 *Select Report*, 579–80.

9 Voter Suppression in the 21st Century

1 "Debunking the Voter Fraud Myth," *Brennan Center for Justice*, January 31, 2017, https://www.brennancenter.org/media/13364/download/briefing_memo_debunking_voter_fraud_myth_0.pdf?inline=1.

2 Lorraine C. Minnite, *The Politics of Voter Fraud*, 2, https://www.projectvote.org/wp-content/uploads/2007/03/Politics_of_Voter_Fraud_Final.pdf?inline=1.

3 Justin Levitt, "A Comprehensive Investigation of Voter Impersonation Finds 31 Credible Incidents out of one Billion Ballots Cast," *Washington Post*, August 6, 2014, https://www.washingtonpost.com/news/wonk/wp/2014/08/06/a-comprehensive-investigation-of-voter-impersonation-finds-31-credible-incidents-out-of-one-billion-ballots-cast/.

4 Some of those studies can be found in "Debunking the Voter Fraud Myth."

5 Eryn J. Newman et al., "Misinformation and the Sins of Memory: False-Belief Formation and Limits on Belief Revision," Journal of Applied Research in Memory and Cognition 11, no. 4 (2021): 471–7.

6 U.S. Senate Republican Policy Committee, *Putting an end to Voter Fraud* (February 15, 2005).

7 Minnite, *The Politics of Voter Fraud*, 5.

8 Hunter Woodall, "Kris Kobach Agrees with Donald Trump that 'millions' Voted Illegally But Offers no Evidence," *Kansas City Star*, November 30, 2016, https://www.kansascity.com/news/politics-government/article117957143.html§orylink=cpy.

9 Ari Berman, "The Man Behind Trump's Voter-Fraud Obsession," *New York Times Magazine*, June 13, 2017.

10 *Crawford vs. Marion County Election Bd*, 553 U.S. 181 (2008).

11 Rick Hase, "Justice Stevens Defends Voter ID Decision Based on Evidence Before Him," *Election Law Blog*, October 17, 2013, https://electionlawblog.org/?p=56071.

12 John Schwartz, "Judge in Landmark Case Disavows Support for Voter ID," *New York Times*, October 15, 2013, https://www.nytimes.com/2013/10/16/us/politics/judge-in-landmark-case-disavows-support-for-voter-id.html?_r=1&adxnnl=1&adxnnlx=1381905375-ED0EgB6Z7qtaGFq7xQ3toQ.

13 *Crawford vs. Marion County Election Bd.*, 472 F. 4th 949, 954 (7th Cir. 2007) (Evans, J., dissenting).

14 Mark Jones et el., *The Texas Voter ID Law and the 2016 Election: A Study of Harris County and Congressional District 23*, Hobby School of Public Affairs, University of Houston (2017), https://uh.edu/hobby/voterid2016/voterid2016.pdf.

15 U.S. Commission on Civil Rights, *An Assessment of Minority Voting Rights Access in the United States (2018)*, https://www.usccr.gov/files/pubs/2018/Minority_Voting_Access_2018.pdf; Zoltan Hajnal, Nazita Lajevardi, and Lindsay Nielson, "Voter Identification Laws and the Suppression of Minority Votes," *Journal of Politics* 79, no. 2 (April 2017): 363.

16 Hajnal, Lajevardi, and Nielson, "Voter Identification Laws," 84.

17 "Voter ID Laws," *NCSL*, updated July 2, 2025, https://www.ncsl.org/elections-and-campaigns/voter-id. NCSL defines "strict" laws as ones in which voters without acceptable identification must vote on a provisional ballot and also take additional steps after Election Day for it to be counted. "Non-strict" laws are those where at least some voters without acceptable identification have an option to cast a ballot that will be counted without further action on the part of the voter.

18 *Hall vs. Holder*, 512 U.S. 874 (1994).

19 *Shelby County vs. Holder*, 570 U.S. 529 (2013).

20 Ari Berman, "Inside John Roberts' Decades-Long Crusade Against the Voting Rights Act," *Politico*, August 10, 2015, https://www.politico.com/magazine/story/2015/08/john-roberts-voting-rights-act-121222/.

21 *North Carolina NAACP vs. McCrory*, 831 F.3d 204, 214, 233 (4th Cir. 2016).

22 Kevin Morris and Coryn Grange, "Growing Racial Disparities in Voter Turnout, 2008–2022," *Brennan Center for Justice*, March 2024, 17, https://www.brennancenter.org/media/12347/download/2024_02_Growing%20Racial_Disparities_in_Voter%20Turnout_Report.pdf?inline=1.

23 Morris and Grange, "Growing Racial Disparities in Voter Turnout, 2008–2022."

24 *Brnovich vs. Democratic Committee*, 594 U.S. 647 (2021).

25 Provisional ballots are required by federal law when poll workers can't determine whether a person is a qualified voter.

26 *Oregon v. Mitchell*, 400 U.S. 112 (1970).

27 Ari Berman, "The Man Behind Trump's Voter-Fraud Obsession," *New York Times Magazine*, June 13, 2017.

28 U.S. Commission on Civil Rights, *An Assessment of Minority Voting Rights*, 152–3, https://www.usccr.gov/files/pubs/2018/Minority_Voting_Access_2018.pdf.

29 In one case True The Vote, well known for voter suppression activities and bogus vote fraud stories, was sued unsuccessfully for voter intimidation in connection with voter challenges. *Fair Fight Inc. vs True The Vote*, 710 F.Supp.3d 1237 (N.D. GA. 2024).

30 U.S. Commission on Civil Rights, *An Assessment of Minority Voting Rights*, 168–78, https://www.usccr.gov/files/pubs/2018/Minority_Voting_Access_2018.pdf.

31 Mark Niesse, "Few Polls Cut Turnout Across Georgia," *Atlanta Journal-Constitution*, December 15. 2019, A1, A19, https://ajc.newspapers.com/image/620200269/?match=1&terms–iesse%20precinct.

32 Many people have the misimpression that non-citizen voting is "unamerican" and has always been illegal. In fact, alien residents were allowed to vote for much of the country's history. Some state constitutions well into the nineteenth century tied voting to residency, not citizenship, and in the middle of that century voting was broadly extended to foreign-born residents who intended to apply for citizenship. See, e.g., *Minor vs. Happersett*, 88 U.S. 162, 177 (1874). It wasn't until the very end of the nineteenth century and the beginning of the twentieth century that nativist politics turned against voting by non-citizens. Arkansas was the last state to repeal its statewide grant of voting rights to non-citizens when it did so in 1926.

33 Michael Waldman, "Advocates for Strict Voting Requirements Can't Find Evidence of Noncitizen Voting," *Brennan Center for Justice*, September 17. 2025, https://www.brennancenter.org/our-work/analysis-opinion/advocates-strict-voting-requirements-cant-find-evidence-noncitizen-voting.

34 North Carolina State Board of Elections, *Election Audit Report*, April 21, 2017, https://s3.amazonaws.com/dl.ncsbe.gov/sboe/Post-lection%20Audit%20Report_2016%20General%20Election/Post-Election_Audit_Report.pdf?utm_source=chatgpt.com.

35 Ben Winslow, "Zero non-citizens voted in Utah review finds," January 23, 2026, https://www.fox13now.com/news/politics/zero-non-citizens-voted-in-utah-review-finds.

36 Iowa reviewed its voter rolls for the 2024 general election and found thirty-five non-citizen ballots out of 1.6 million cast (approximately 0.002%) and noted that many voters flagged as non-citizens were actually people who had naturalized. Hannah Fingerhut, "Iowa review finds 35 noncitizens voted last fall. That is a tiny fraction of the ballots cast," March 20, 2025, *AP News*, https://apnews.com/article/iowa-noncitizen-voting-1badfb99ab7ef21a6fb176d2867d51e5. A Reuters survey of state and private reviews found that instances of non-citizen voting were "extremely rare." See https://www.reuters.com/world/us/noncitizen-voters-rarity-us-elections-state-private-reviews-show-2024-10-03/?utm_source=chatgpt.com.

37 Alex Nowrasteh, "Noncitizens Don't Illegally Vote in Detectable Numbers," *Cato at Liberty*, November 25, 2020, https://www.cato.org/blog/noncitizens-dont-illegally-vote-detectable-numbers. The *Cato* report also debunked a 2014 study by Jesse Richman that had claimed that 6.4 and 2.2 percent of non-citizens voted in the 2008 and 2010 elections, respectively. Others have also shown that Richman's methodology and conclusions were nonsense, but vote suppressors continue to rely on it.

38 Ian Vandewalker. "Analysis: The Effects of Requiring Documentary Proof of Citizenship To Register To Vote," *Brennan Center for Justice*, https://www.brennancenter.org/sites/default/files/2021-09/Requiring%20Citizenship%20to%20Register%20to%20Vote.pdf.

39 *Mi Familia Vota vs. Fontes*, 129 F.4th 691 (2025), stay granted in part, 145 S. Ct. 108 (2024).

40 Citizenship has been exploited in other efforts to increase Republican representation. The first Trump administration tried, unsuccessfully, to undercount immigrants in the 2020 census in order to give more congressional seats to conservative states that had fewer immigrants. *Department of Commerce vs. New York*, 588 US 752 (2019). The Constitution requires congressional apportionment to be based on the "whole number of persons in each state" regardless of citizenship, but conservatives have argued that states are required to redistrict their own legislatures based on the number of eligible voters alone. The Supreme Court rejected that claim but left open the question of whether a state could voluntarily choose to do so. *Evenwel vs. Abbott*, 578 U.S. 54 (2016).

10 The Next Stolen Election

1 Alan Feurer et al., "Trump Demands That Bondi Move 'Now' to Prosecute Foes," *New York Times*, September 21, 2025, https://www.nytimes.com/2025/09/20/us/politics/trump-justice-department-us-attorneys.html.

2 Glenn Thrush, "Trump Names More Foes He Wants Prosecuted as Bondi and Patel Look On," *New York Times*, October 15, 2025, https://www.nytimes.com/2025/10/15/us/politics/trump-bondi-patel-blanche-oval-office.html.

3 Devlin Barrett, "Justice Dept. Official Pushes Prosecutors to Investigate George Soros's Foundation," *New York Times*, September 25, 2025, https://www.nytimes.com/2025/09/25/us/politics/justice-trump-george-soros-foundation.html.

4 James Poniewozik, "The F.C.C. Threatened to Punish Kimmel 'the Hard Way.' ABC Made It Easy," *New York Times*, September 18, 2025, https://www.nytimes.com/2025/09/18/arts/television/jimmy-kimmel.html.

5 Peter Baker, "In Assault on Free Speech, Trump Targets Speech He Hates," *New York Times*, September 21, 2025, https://www.nytimes.com/2025/09/21/us/politics/trump-free-speech.html.

6 Luke Broadwater, "Trump Says Critical Coverage of Him Is 'Really Illegal,'" *New York Times*, September 19, 2025, https://www.nytimes.com/2025/09/19/us/politics/trump-media-news-free-speech.html.

7 *Illinois vs. Trump*, 155 F.4th 929, 939 (7th Cir.), stay denied, 146 S. Ct. 432 (2025).

8 *Trump vs. United States*, 603 U.S. 593 (2024). Once again, the conservative justices' platitudes about "strict construction" were ignored to achieve the result they wanted. There isn't *one word* in the Constitution that hints that presidents are above the law or immune from prosecution for any crime. It's strange for Americans to see ex-President Yoon of South Korea sentenced to life imprisonment for insurrection, and to see a member of the English royal family arrested for "misconduct in public office." For two-and-a-half centuries, Americans prided themselves that no one was above the law, but that revered principle was shattered by the court's decision.

9 Britain Eakin, "Request for Voter Information Spurs Legal Woes for Kobach," *Courthouse News Service*, July 2017, https://api.courthousenews.com/request-voter-information-spurs-legal-woes-kobach/.

10 As of this writing, lower courts have generally ruled in favor of states that have refused to give voter information to the DOJ. See, e.g., *United States of America vs. Benson*, ___ F.Supp. 3d ___ (W.D. Michigan, January 20, 2026); *United States of America vs. State of Oregon*, ___ F.Supp. 3d ___ (D. Oregon February 5, 2026) (Because of the DOJ's repeated misrepresentations, the trial judge wrote that that the "presumption of regularity . . . that [the DOJ] could be taken at its word—with little doubt about its intentions and stated purposes—no longer holds.")

11 Chris Cameron, "Bannon claims 'there is a plan' for Trump to run for a third term," *New York Times*, October 24, 2025, https://www.nytimes.com/2025/10/24/us/politics/president-trump-2028-steve-bannon.html.

12 Conservative estimates show that the Trump family has made more than $1.4 billion by exploiting the second term of his presidency. Nicholas Kristof, " What Trump Is the Best at, Hands Down," *New York Times*, February 11, 2026, https://www.nytimes.com/2026/02/11/opinion/trump-crypto-corruption.html.

13 *Trump vs. Anderson*, 601 U.S. 100 (2024).

14 *American Assoc. of University Professors vs. Rubio*, 802 F.Supp.3d 120 (D. Mass. 2025).

BIBLIOGRAPHY

Anderson, Carol. *One Person, No Vote: How Voter Suppression is Destroying Our Democracy*. New York: Bloomsbury Publishing, 2018.

Anderson, William. *The Wild Man From Sugar Creek: The Political Career of Eugene Talmadge*. Baton Rouge: Louisiana State University Press, 1975.

Berman, Ari. *Give Us The Ballot: The Modern Struggle for Voting Rights in America*. New York: Farrar, Straus and Giroux, 2015.

Bolton, John. *The Room Where It Happened: A Whitehouse Memoir*. New York: Simon & Schuster, 2020.

Boulard, Garry. *Daniel Sickles: A Life*. Bloomington, IN: iUniverse, 2019.

Bullock, Charles S., Scott E. Buchanan, and Ronald Keith Geddie. *The Three Governors' Controversy: Skullduggery, Machinations, and the Decline of Georgia's Progressive Politics*. Athens: University of Georgia Press, 2015.

Caro, Robert A. *The Years of Lyndon Johnson: Means of Ascent*. New York: Vintage Books, 1990.

Caro, Robert A. *The Years of Lyndon Johnson: The Path to Power*. New York: Vintage Books, 1981.

Carter, Jimmy, *Turning Point: A Candidate, a State, and a Nation Come of Age*. New York: Random House, 1992.

Catt, Carrie Chapman and Nettie Rogers Shuler. *Woman Suffrage & Politics: The Inner Story of the Suffrage Movement*. New York: Charles Scribner's Sons, 1923.

Dallek, Robert. *Lonestar Rising: Lyndon Johnson and His Times 1908–1960*. New York: Oxford University Press, 1991.

Dershowitz, Alan M. *Supreme Injustice: How the High Court Hijacked Election 2000*. New York: Oxford University Press, 2001.

Engstrom, Erik J. *Partisan Gerrymandering and the Construction of American Democracy*. Ann Arbor: University of Michigan Press, 2016.

Haberman, Maggie. *Confidence Man: The Making of Donald Trump and the Breaking of America*. New York: Penguin Press, 2022.

Hasen, Richard L. *The Voting Wars: From Florida 2000 to the Next Election Meltdown*. New Haven, CT: Yale University Press, 2012.

Keena, Alex, Michael Latner, Anthony J. McGann, and Charles Anthony Smith. *Gerrymandering the States: Partisanship, Race and the Transformation of American Federalism*. New York: Cambridge University Press, 2021.

Kousser, J. Morgan. *The Shaping of Southern Politics: Suffrage Restriction and the Establishment of the One-Party South 1880–1910*. New Haven, CT: Yale University Press, 1974.

Kranish, Michael and Marc Fisher, *Trump Revealed: The Definitive Biography of the 45th President*. New York: Scribner, 2016.

Lichtman, Allan J. *The Embattled Vote in America: From the Founding to the Present.* Cambridge, MA: Harvard University Press, 2018.

Morris, Roy Jr. *Fraud of the Century.* New York: Simon & Schuster, 2003.

Raven, Rory. *The Dorr War: Treason, Rebellion & The Fight for Reform in Rhode Island.* Charleston, SC: The History Press, 2003.

Seabrook, Nick. *One Person, One Vote: A Surprising History of Gerrymandering in America.* New York: Pantheon Books, 2022.

Sternstein, Jerome L. "The Sickles Memorandum: Another Look at the Hayes–Tilden Election-Night Conspiracy." *Journal of Southern History* 342, no. 32 (August 1966).

Tapper, Jake. *Down & Dirty: The Plot to Steal the Presidency.* New York: Little, Brown and Company, 2001.

Toobin, Jeffrey. *Too Close to Call: The Thirty-six-Day Battle to Decide the 2000 Election.* New York: Random House Trade Paperbacks, 2001.

Woodward, C. Vann. *Reunion and Reaction: The Compromise of 1877 and the End of Reconstruction.* New York: Oxford University Press, 1951.

Woodward, C. Vann. *The Strange Career of Jim Crow.* New York: Oxford University Press, 1955.

INDEX

Index for *Stealing Elections, American Style* by Christine Graham 1 April 2026 (1010 lines)